M000209096

"Stan is the sherpa that guides ex the heart and mind of business stakeholders. Stakeholders aren't always customers though. At a time when company vision and culture matters more than ever, it takes inspired and engaged employees to bring them to life."

- **Brian Solis**, author of *What's the Future of Business #WTF, The End of Business as Usual* and *Engage!*

"So often overlooked, and so very vital to building company value... empowering employees to support each other and the brand. For our team at Collective Bias, it's about being socially connected in as many ways as possible... from all wearing Nike Fuel Bands to using PATH as our company intranet. Stan Phelps 'gets' it and Green Goldfish will walk you step-by-step though achieving this critical goal."

- **Ted Rubin**, author of *Return on Relationship*

"Great customer centric organizations only exist because of engaged and empowered employees. The Green Goldfish is packed with awesome examples of what world class companies are doing today to inspire and reward their employees. If you see value in truly building an "A Team," Green Goldfish will be, without question, your single best reference."

- **Chris Zane**, Founder and President of Zane's Cycles, author of *Reinventing the Wheel, the Science of Creating Lifetime Customers*

"Stan Phelps takes customer service to a whole new level by focusing on EMPLOYEE service, and how to do well by your employees - so they take care of your customers. Packed with stories, insights and R.U.L.E.S. any company can follow, this book is a must-read for managers of companies of all shapes and sizes who know that employees don't leave jobs - they leave managers, especially when they don't feel your love and appreciation. Pick this up, and start engaging your team and making more GREEN!

- **Phil Gerbyshak**, author of *The Naked Truth of Social Media*

"If you're looking for ways to inspire your employees to love your company, and if you're smart enough to realize that money can't buy you love, then you need real-life, uber-successful examples from real-life, uber-profitable companies. Look no farther! In your hands, you've got examples from hundreds and hundreds of companies."

- **Ted Coiné**, author of *Five Star Customer Service* and *Spoil 'Em Rotten!*

"Our large-scale research shows unequivocally that engaged employees are more likely to work longer, try harder, make more suggestions for improvement, recruit others to join their company, and go out of their way to help customers. They even take less sick time. Companies can tap into the enormous value of engaged employees by following the 15 ideas that Stan lays out in this book."

- **Bruce Temkin**, author of *The Six Laws of Customer Experience*

"Too often, the actual employment experience delivered on the job does not measure up to the version sold to job candidates during the interview process. In *What's Your Green Goldfish*, Stan Phelps offers 15 ways to close the gap."

- **Steve Curtin**, author of *Delight Your Customers: 7 Simple Ways to Raise Your Customer Service from Ordinary to Extraordinary* (AMACOM, June 2013)

"In *What's Your Green Goldfish*, Stan Phelps brilliantly applies the idea of 'doing a little something extra' for employees. You know, those people that actually get the work done and keep customers happy. Read it, put some of the ideas to work, and soon you'll be reaping more 'green' from your customers."

- **Bob Thompson**, Founder and CEO, CustomerThink Corp.

"*What's Your Green Goldfish* shows how to manage employees by commitment and not control. Bravo!"

- **Barry Moltz**, author of *Bounce*, *Crazy!* and *B-A-M*

WHAT'S YOUR GREEN GOLDFISH

BEYOND DOLLARS: 15 WAYS TO DRIVE EMPLOYEE ENGAGEMENT AND REINFORCE CULTURE

This book is dedicated to the memory of my mother
Pauline Dora Phelps. The first person to believe
in me and encourage me to follow my dreams.

Published by 9 INCH MARKETING, LLC
Cary, North Carolina

Editing: Jennifer Phelps, Sharon E. Reed and Keith Green
Cover Design: Matthew Sinegal

ISBN: 978-0-9849838-1-0

First Printing: 2013 Printed in the United States of America

What's Your Green Goldfish is available for bulk orders, special promotions and premiums. For details call +1.919.360.4702 or e-mail stan@9inchmarketing.com.

TABLE OF CONTENTS

PART I:
WHAT IS A GREEN GOLDFISH?

PART II:
THE 5 INGREDIENTS OR R.U.L.E.S.
OF A GREEN GOLDFISH

PART III:
THE 15 TYPES OF GREEN GOLDFISH

FOREWORD
by Ted Coiné

*"No, a Green Goldfish does not have to cost your
company a single penny. It isn't about the money.
You can't buy your employees' love, no matter how much you spend.
But you sure can invest in it, as the examples in this book attest."*

For years now, I've been sharing a basic truth with my audiences and readers: *In business, doing the right thing pays.*

You can call this good karma or following the Golden Rule if you choose. For those of you who are more pragmatic, you can chalk it up to savvy business sense. Whether you're focused on the first half of this proposition (*doing the right thing*) or the second (*pays*), my role is to drive this message home in a way my print and real-life audiences can taste, feel, and ultimately buy into. Because let's face it: you can tell someone the truth until your throat is raw. Until they own it for themselves, you're wasting your time, and theirs.

Fortunately, even the most intelligent of we humans respond well to two types of new information: that which is simple, and real-life examples.

So imagine my delight when my friend Stan Phelps began his Goldfish projects a few years ago! Every day, it seemed, he would post on his blog a new example of what he called marketing lagniappe, or the little things that make a world of difference. He set out to collect 1,001 examples, and asked his robust social media network for help.

The results of this initial (brilliantly crowd sourced) research are available in his first book, *What's Your Purple Goldfish*. Chances are good you've already read it, and you're back now for a deeper dive.

"Deeper?" Absolutely. *Purple Goldfish* is all about customer service. His premise is simple and, to anyone who's owned or run a business, inescapable: spoil your customers rotten, surprise them with a little extra that they can't get anywhere else, and they're yours for life. Better, their friends will be, too, because there's nothing we humans enjoy more than sharing stories – good or bad – with our friends. Give your customers an irresistible story to share about how wonderful your company is, and they'll become your most effective sales force. The *Purple Goldfish Project* provides 1,001 such stories, about almost as many companies.

So that's his *Purple Goldfish* book, and if you haven't read it, read it next. But I claim his *Green Goldfish* book – this one – takes you one deeper. Here's how:

With the right practices in place, with good training and tight-as-a-drum supervision, even the most draconian of managements can achieve winning customer service that wows customers. I hate to admit that, but I've seen it with my own eyes, so I have to be honest. Fortunately, it's beyond rare that a company can pull this off. It's just too exhausting to maintain with any consistency. Customers can sense employee misery, even through forced smiles, and it turns them off.

What turns customers *on* is sincerity: employee *love* of their company: engagement, in other words. That is where the *Green Goldfish* book comes in – yes, the one you hold in your hands right now!

If you're looking for ways to inspire your employees to love your company, and if you're smart enough to realize that money can't buy you love, then you need real-life, uber-successful examples from real-life, uber-profitable companies. Look no farther! In your hands, you've got examples from hundreds and hundreds of companies. Some are firms you already know. For instance:

- **Facebook** gives employees a $4,500 bonus for having a baby – just when they need it most!

- **Patagonia** makes the world – and employees' lives – better through two weeks' paid time off to work in the green nonprofit of their choice.
- **Intel** has greeters and gifts awaiting new hires. What a way to start a new career!

Others are ones you've likely never heard of, but should know well, including:

- **Realflow** engages employees through smoothie competitions. Taste and healthy ingredients are included in judging criteria.
- **Tarbar**'s Thumbs Up Award is a roaming desktop statue employees can earn by doing something above and beyond the call of job performance.
- **AnswerLab**'s employees can each schedule one-on-one time with their CEO to "walk and talk" - literally. He goes for a walk with each one!

If you notice, some of these Green Goldfish companies invest green – that is, money – in ways that show their employees how important they are to the company. The first three examples all fit into this category. A little bit of money, invested meaningfully, can indeed get your point across quite well.

But if you also notice, you don't have to spend a dime in order to get this message through (and as a pathologically frugal former CEO myself, this really works for me!). How much do smoothie ingredients cost? How much does one roaming award cost?

… And my favorite of the list, the walk and talk with the CEO? Last time I checked, walking was free. Free, but priceless! As most readers of my blog, SwitchandShift.com, are well aware, I have a special place in my heart – and most posts – for the power of Management By Walking Around: and the more casual the walking (or eating), the more likely important, company-improving issues will bubble to the top where something can be done about them.

No, a Green Goldfish does not have to cost your company a single penny. It isn't about the money. Green Goldfish — and the green of profits — they're all about employee engagement, employee love. You can't buy your employees' love, no matter how much you spend. But you sure can invest in it, as the 200+ examples in this book attest.

I'd like to close this forward with a quote from an employee at another of the Green Goldfish companies, the SAS Institute:

> *"You're given the freedom, the flexibility, and the resources to do your job. Because if you're treated well, you treat the company well."*

Doing the right thing pays. *What's Your Green Goldfish* is your how-to manual to make this essential business truth come to life at your company. Buy it. Read it. Share it. Most importantly, do it.

You'll thank me for this advice. You'll thank Stan Phelps for this book.

- Ted Coiné
Former CEO, Speaker and Business Heretic
Author of *Five Star Customer Service* and *Spoil 'Em Rotten!*

INTRODUCTION

*"I came to see in my time at IBM that 'culture' isn't
just one aspect of the game – it is the game."*

- Lou Gerstner, Former IBM CEO, Author of
Who Says Elephants Can't Dance

HAPPY EMPLOYEES CREATE HAPPY CUSTOMERS

I recently completed a quest. I had set out to find 1,001 purple goldfish. Examples of companies that strive to exceed customer expectations via a sticky concept called **g.l.u.e.** (giving little unexpected extras) Signature extras that help win customers and influence word of mouth.

What became clear during my research is that most brands who practice marketing g.l.u.e. for customers, also embrace the concept with employees. Taking care of employees and investing in the "little extras" for staff helps build a dynamic culture.

Here is a great quote by Vince Burks of Amica Insurance {Endnote 1} explaining this exact focus,

> *At Amica Insurance – the concept of lagniappe is not just a part of our brand ethos; it is ingrained in everything we do. It therefore extends to our most valued resource – our employees. In fact, that is the secret to our success.*

> *Excellent benefits. Advancement opportunities. The latest technology. A real work/life balance. And an open and regular line of communication with each other and with senior management. Taken together, we give our employees all that they need to succeed ... and more.*

> *This is absolutely essential. Satisfied employees lead to*

satisfied customers. Long-term employees lead to long term relationships with customers. And pride, trust, and morale are all contagious.

Further, well-trained, long-term employees know how to get the job done quickly, efficiently, and effectively. They know their customers. They know their colleagues. They know their company. And they therefore know how to "get to yes" with ease and a sense of grace. This is good for the customer. This is good for the company.

This book is the culmination of my most recent quest in the goldfish trilogy. A collection of 1,001 examples of green goldfish. Why green for employees? First and foremost, green is one of the three colors of Mardi Gras (purple, green and gold). New Orleans is the birthplace of lagniappe, the overarching concept for "giving little unexpected extras." The second reason deals with money. Studies show financial compensation is not a strong long-term motivator for employee engagement {Endnote 2}. Money can be more of a hindrance than help. The final reason is that Green is about growth. When you are green, you are growing. When you are ripe, you begin to rot. Green goldfish are the little things that can make the big difference in establishing a strong corporate culture.

Similar to the concept of Purple Goldfish, it is my belief that employee lagniappe provides the following three benefits:

1. Differentiation – a way to stand out in a sea of sameness. Give the company a remark-able difference or set of signature differences.

2. Retention – keep employees happy and they tend to stick around longer.

3. Word of Mouth – create a culture that attracts talent. Become a desired place to work and you'll get more "A" players.

PROLOGUE

TOWELS AND HAMMERS

*"Our people are our single greatest strength and
most enduring long-term competitive advantage."*

- Gary Kelly, Southwest Airlines CEO

A TALE OF TWO GIANTS

In 2011, Google was crowned the "HAPPIEST COMPANY IN AMERICA" by CareerBliss.com {Endnote 3}. The rankings are based on 100,000+ worker-generated reviews spanning over 10,000 companies. Scores were based on such factors as work-life balance, relationships with bosses and co-workers, compensation, growth opportunities, a company's culture and the opportunity for employees to exert control over the daily workflow.

Google didn't become a happy company by mistake. It's a product of thoughtful design and ultimately culture. Founders Larry Page and Sergey Brin set the groundwork for building Google. Here are some telling quotes by Page in a recent New York Times post {Endnote 4}:

> *"We have somewhat of a social mission, and most other companies do not. I think that's why people like working for us, and using our services...Companies' goals should be to make their employees so wealthy that they do not need to work, but choose to because they believe in the company... Hopefully, I believe in a world of abundance, and in that world, many of our employees don't have to work, they're pretty wealthy and they could probably go years without working. Why are they working? They're working because they like doing something, they believe in what they're doing."*

But maybe there is a deeper reason for creating a more welcoming and fulfilling workplace. Here is a quote from CEO Larry Page's Commencement Address {Endnote 5} at the University of Michigan in May 2009:

> "My father's father worked in the Chevy plant in Flint, Michigan. He was an assembly line worker...My Grandpa used to carry an "Alley Oop" hammer – a heavy iron pipe with a hunk of lead melted on the end. The workers made them during the sit-down strikes to protect themselves. When I was growing up, we used that hammer whenever we needed to pound a stake or something into the ground. It is wonderful that most people don't need to carry a heavy blunt object for protection anymore. But just in case, I have it here."

(Image Credit: YouTube)

It bears repeating. **Larry Page's grandfather used to take a hammer to work for protection**. A lead pipe with a hunk of metal melted on the end of it. I can only imagine this was a constant reminder of the quest for a happy workplace at Google.

THROWING IN THE TOWELS

As part of a broad series of cutbacks in 2004, Microsoft eliminated the laundered towel service. The towels were available for employees who showered after biking to work or playing sports on the company's Redmond campus. That and the other changes, especially to the employee stock purchase program, caused a groundswell of opposition from a majority of Microsoft employees. The towels became a rallying point of discontent. {Seattle PI Endnote 6}

According to the blog mini Microsoft, {Endnote 7}

> *"It's not like we're sweaty work-out animals always in need of a shower and fresh towel. No. What riled us was the bone-headed way the towel cut-back was handled, explained, and justified. It truly made us wonder just who are these people in charge and just who do they think they are leading? The towels became the symbol of poor leadership."*

Rancor continued and some prominent departures from Microsoft ensued. Business Week {Endnote 8} reported about troubling exits, "Just whisper the word 'towels' to any Microsoft employee, and eyes roll. Employees who helped the company build its huge cash stockpile were furious."

Less than two years later the towels were back. Microsoft reinstated the laundered towel service and added additional extras in an effort to stem the tide of exits and increase morale.

PREFACE

*"It is our belief that work/life balance should be
in the hands of the employee and that
happy, balanced people make better employees."*

-Janelle Raney, Citrix

THE WORKPLACE IS CHANGING

One could make the assertion that workplace has changed more in the last five years than it has in the previous 25. Seismic shifts in technology, social media and management have drastically changed how we work. Combine all this change with record levels of disengagement, meaning employees are emotionally disconnected from their workplaces and are less likely to be productive. According to Gallup, over 23 million U.S. workers are actively disengaged. {Endnote 9}

Let's look at a Top 10 list of compelling reasons to invest in employee engagement:

10. Dollars and sense

If organizations increased investment in a range of
good workplace practices related to engagement by just **10**%,
they would increase profits by $2,400 per employee. {IES / Work Foundation Report Endnote 10}

Less than one in **10** middle managers deemed the quality of
their management training to be excellent. {Accenture Endnote 11}

9. People are people

Engagement and involvement are critical in managing change at work; **9** out of 10 of the key barriers to the success of change programs are people related. {PwC Endnote 12}

Seventy-five percent of leaders have no engagement plan or strategy even though **90**% say engagement impacts business success. {ACCOR Endnote 13}

8. Triple your pleasure

Engaged organizations grew profits as much as three times faster than their competitors. According to a report by the Corporate Leadership Council, highly engaged organizations have the potential to reduce staff turnover by **87**% and improve performance by 20%. {Corporate Leadership Council Endnote 14}

7. I've got a problem with my boss

75%-80% of people leave jobs because of relationship issues. {Saratoga Institute Endnote 15}

75% of people voluntarily leaving jobs don't quit their jobs; they quit their bosses. {Roger Herman Endnote 16}

6. Is it ignorance or apathy?

I don't know and I don't care. **69**% of US employees are either "not engaged," or are "actively disengaged." {Gallup Endnote 17}

5. What's your Return on Engagement?

Less than **50%** of Chief Financial Officers appear to understand the return on their investments in human capital. {Accenture Endnote 18}

4. Show me the plan

Based on a recent study by Chris Zook, the co-head of the Worldwide Strategy Practice at Bain & Company, only **40%** of the workforce knew about the corporation's goals, strategies and tactics. {Bain Endnote 19}

3. Recognition matters

43% of highly engaged employees receive feedback at least once a week compared to only 18% of employees with low engagement. {Towers Watson Endnote 20}

2. Moving the needle

Earnings per share (EPS) growth of 89 organizations found that the EPS growth rate of organizations with engagement scores in the top quartile was **2**.6 times that of organizations with below-average engagement scores. {Gallup Endnote 21}

... and the #1 reason for paying attention to employee engagement:

1. Sincerity and trust

Of seventy-five possible drivers of engagement the **ONE** that was rated as the most important was the extent to which employees believed that their senior management had a sincere interest in their well-being. {Towers Watson Endnote 22}

PART I:

WHAT IS A GREEN GOLDFISH?

Chapter 1

EMPLOYEES FIRST

*"Employees First, Customers Second is a management approach.
It is a philosophy, a set of ideas, a way of looking
at strategy and competitive advantage."*

– Vineet Nayar, CEO HCL Technologies

THE MOST IMPORTANT TWO FEET IN MARKETING

Where is value created in an enterprise? It's created in the last two feet of a transaction, the space between the employee and the customer.

In 2005, HCL Technologies of India {Endnote 23} needed a transformational change. New CEO Vineet Nayar decided to make a statement. He set out a new strategy focusing on "Employees First."

Vineet understood the importance of interactions between front line employees and the customer. He calls these 24 inches the "value zone." The priority at HCL became: Employees first, customers second, management third and shareholders last. His employees on the front line were the key to the turnaround of HCL. They were the true custodians of the brand and drivers of customer loyalty. Nayar wanted to shift the focus from the "WHAT" of what HCL offered, to the "HOW" of delivering value.

HCL decided to turn conventional management upside down. They inverted the pyramid and placed employees first. This wasn't just lip service. Vineet engaged in a number of changes that reinforced the new direction. These changes became beacons along the voyage, helping to drive employee engagement and reinforce culture. Nayar drew his inspiration from Mohatma Gandhi and his famous Dandi March. Mahatma walked to the sea to make salt as a protest to the

British government and their monopoly on salt production in India. This small action ignited change, becoming a catalyst that led to a large scale uprising.

Nayar knew he needed actions and not words. Here are some of the "green goldfish" changes HCL Technologies made on their journey:

OPENING THE WINDOW OF INFORMATION

HCL (#809) put together an online forum for employees called U&I. Employees could ask any question to the senior team at HCL Technologies. It was an open site where everyone could see the question, the questioner, and the answer. Employees responded favorably as noted by this comment,

> "This is the biggest change we have seen at HCL in years. Now we have a management team that is willing to acknowledge the dirt."

Why open the window of information? Vineet uses the analogy of an Amsterdam Window. Having previously lived on the Herengracht ("Gentleman's Canal") in Amsterdam, I can attest that these windows are immense. They are a throwback to the modest Calvinist period {Endnote 24} when subtle expressions of wealth, such as being able to afford to pay the highest window tax, were favored by the rich. In the words of writer Joanna Tweedy, "Today, the centuries-old glass, beautifully imperfect, frames the olive-green waters outside and lets natural light, and the eyes of curious tourists, pour in."

While visiting Amsterdam, Vineet pointed to windows and asked his friend, "Why so large?" The friend mentioned all the obvious reasons like letting in light and enjoying the view of the canal, but then offered a much more interesting answer... "It keeps the house clean." It turns out that the bigger your windows, the more glass you have, the more visible your dirt will be - to you and to everyone who visits or passes by.

In Vineet's words,

> *"If you can see the dirt, you will be much more likely to get rid of it. A transparent house has a dramatic effect on the culture inside."*

TRUST PAY

Vineet developed a clear point of view on compensation and recognition during his twenty years with HCL. "The industry used to pay 30 per cent variable compensation to the employee linked to the company's performance." He found the idea quite ridiculous, because if you are a software engineer you have no meaningful influence on the performance of the company. So HCL turned that amount into fixed pay – "trust pay." It allowed HCL to start focusing on the value employees were creating for the customer.

OPEN 360-DEGREE REVIEW

To help invert the organizational pyramid, **HCL** (#938) opened the 360-degree performance review process to all employees who a manager might influence and allowed anyone who had given a manager feedback access to the results of that manager's 360. This practice increased participation, empowered employees, and made the 360-review a development tool, not an evaluative one.

HCL RESULTS: Faced with one of the toughest recessions in recent history, HCL Technologies called on the talents and insights of its employees and became one of the fastest growing companies in the world.

OVERALL TAKEAWAY: Culture trumps strategy and principles beat rules. The entire premise of *What's Your Green Goldfish* is that employees must come first. Employee experience should be priority Numero Uno.

Chapter 2

BUILDING FOR RETENTION

"One thing that always surprised me in prior work experiences is when your assets walk out the door each day, why aren't companies doing more to value the people doing the business?"

- Robert Murray, CEO iProspect

WHO IS MORE IMPORTANT... EMPLOYEES OR CUSTOMERS?

This is a great chicken and egg question with regard to leadership. Who comes first? What became clear during my research is that brands who understand the concept of lagniappe for customers, also embrace the concept with employees. Both are equally important. Taking care of employees and investing into the "little extras" for staff help build a dynamic culture.

What type of company do you want to be when you grow up?

About seven years ago I had the chance to cross paths with a friend from college. Tom Coyne and I had lived on the same floor our freshman year at Marist College. Tom captained the football team, brandishing a personality and a warm smile that lit up a room.

Tom was now a successful businessman, owning his own agency. Coyne Public Relations was based in Parsippany, NJ and boasted an impressive list of clients. Tom and his team worked with iconic brands such as Disney, Campbell Soup and Burger King.

While sitting down with Tom, I had the opportunity to ask him about his business philosophy. He relayed an approach that has stuck with me to this day. It was both simple and prophetic. I'll paraphrase his words,

"When I started the agency, my goal was not to be the biggest or to have the best clients. It was simply to become the best agency to work for. I knew if we were the best agency to work for, we would then attract the best people. And that if we retained the best people, the best clients will follow."

It's been over two decades since Tom Coyne started his agency as a sole proprietor. The firm now boasts over 110 employees and maintains offices in both Parsippany and New York City.

In 2009, Coyne was named the "*Best Agency to Work for in America*" by The Holmes Report. {Endnote 25} In addition, this past year Coyne became a finalist for PR Week's *Mid-Size Agency of the Year*. No surprise here as Coyne has dominated the Small Agency category for the better part of a decade. It's only a matter of time before Coyne begins to give the large agencies some additional competition.

How does Coyne focus on becoming the best?

Coyne focuses on putting its employees first. Supporting employees by promoting a work/life balance. Allowing team members not only to make a great living, but allowing them to enjoy a strong quality of life. The best companies like Coyne PR are places where employees are truly excited about coming in every day.

Here are some green goldfish from Coyne:

> #817 - Coyne College is the agency's internal training program. The program is designed to develop the knowledge and skills of Coyne's employees and give them the best opportunity to succeed, wherever their careers take them. Beyond Coyne College, the agency encourages employees to seek additional ways to continue their education and further their understanding of public relations and their clients' industries.

#847 - As part of designing the new offices at Coyne PR's HQ in NJ, the senior team polled the employees for suggestions. The result: *The Zen Den*, a room for relaxation. Totally painted in black, with massage chairs and a Fish Tank video screen. It's a perfect place to unwind and rejuvenate.

#848 - Coyne has a nail salon in its office. Once a week it is open for employees free of charge.

#851 - *Winter Friday's*. In lieu of a formal company holiday party, Coyne PR recently decided to focus on employees for the entire month of December. One of the favorite activities was Winter Friday's. The entire firm received Friday's off for the month of December. On 12-12-12, the agency surprised everyone by shuttling the whole agency over to the mall mid-morning. Each employee was given $250 on one condition: the money needed to be spent on only themselves. All food and beverage at the mall was covered. Employees could go anywhere they pleased and just drop their business card for payment. The day ended back at Coyne PR headquarters for food and drinks for the entire staff.

SHIFTING YOUR MINDSET

Employees are the bedrock of your organization. You would be better served taking compensation out of the equation and thinking of them as volunteers. Here is a great analysis from Ted Coiné on this exact approach:

> *"CEOs, team leaders, and everyone in between: if your people don't LOVE your company after four years of employment (or four months, or four quarters), that's all on you... Do you have the pick of the employment litter? Are your best people dying to stay on board? If not, it isn't that they're ungrateful, and it isn't that your competitors are luring them away. It's that you suck as a leader... Act as if every*

single employee is a volunteer. Because you know what? In a fundamental way, they are." {Endnote 26}

TAKEAWAY: Focus on what you can control, creating a great environment to work in. That environment or culture will then attract the best people.

Chapter 3

WHY GREEN AND WHY A GOLDFISH?

"It has long been an axiom of mine that the little things are infinitely the most important."

– Sir Arthur Conan Doyle

GOLDFISH ON THE BRAIN

OK – I'll be the first to admit it. I am oddly preoccupied with goldfish. Mainly because the average common goldfish is four inches, yet the largest in the world is almost five times that size! {Endnote 27}

Five Times Larger!!! Imagine walking down the street and bumping into someone 25 feet tall. How can there be such a disparity between ordinary goldfish and their monster cousins? Part of my obsession is my firm belief that growing a successful culture is similar to the growth of a goldfish.

Let's break down a green goldfish into two parts:

WHY A GOLDFISH?

It turns out that the growth of a goldfish is determined by five factors:

#1. Size of the Environment = The Market
GROWTH FACTOR: The size of the bowl or pond.

> *RULE OF THUMB: Direct correlation. The larger the bowl or pond, the larger the goldfish can grow. The smaller the market, the lesser the growth.*

#2. Number of Goldfish = Competition

GROWTH FACTOR: The number of goldfish in the same bowl or pond.

> *RULE OF THUMB: Inverse correlation. The more goldfish, the less growth. The less competition, the more growth opportunity.*

#3. The Quality of the Water = The Culture

GROWTH FACTOR: The clarity and amount of nutrients in the water.

> *RULE OF THUMB: Direct correlation. The better the quality, the larger the growth.*

FACT: A MALNOURISHED GOLDFISH IN A CROWDED, CLOUDY ENVIRONMENT MAY ONLY GROW TO TWO INCHES (5 CM).

#4. How they're treated the first 120 days of life = Onboarding

GROWTH FACTOR: The nourishment and treatment they receive as a fry (baby goldfish).

> *RULE OF THUMB: Direct correlation. The lower the quality of the food, water and treatment, the more the goldfish will be stunted for future growth. The stronger the culture and support, the better the growth.*

#5. Genetic Make-up = Differentiation

GROWTH FACTOR: The genetic make-up of the goldfish.

RULE OF THUMB: Direct correlation. The poorer the genes or the less differentiated, the less the goldfish can grow. The more differentiated the product or service (culture) from the competition, the better the chance for growth.

FACT: THE CURRENT *GUINNESS BOOK OF WORLD RECORDS* HOLDER FOR THE LARGEST GOLDFISH HAILS FROM THE NETHERLANDS AT A LENGTHY 19 INCHES / 50 CM.

Which of the five factors can you control?

Let's assume you have an existing product or service and have been in business for more than six months. Do you have any control over the market, your competition or the economy? NO, NO and NO. The only thing you have control over is your business' genetic make-up or how you create your culture. In goldfish terms, how do you stand out in a sea of sameness?

WHY GREEN?

#1. Lagniappe is **creole** for "*a little something extra.*" Green is an ode to the birthplace of the word [New Orleans] and the colors of its most famous event [Mardi Gras].

The accepted story behind the original selection of the Mardi Gras colors {Endnote 28} originates from 1872 when the Grand Duke Alexis Romanoff of Russia visited New Orleans. It is said that the Grand Duke came to the city in pursuit of an actress named Lydia Thompson. During his stay, he was given the honor of selecting the official Mardi Gras colors by the Krewe of Rex. His selection of purple, green and gold would also later become the colors of the House of Romanoff.

The 1892 Rex Parade theme first gave meaning to the official Mardi Gras colors. Inspired by New Orleans and the traditional colors, purple was symbolic of justice, green was symbolic of faith and gold was symbolic of power.

#2. Money is not a motivator. According to McKinsey, {Endnote 29} numerous studies have shown that for people with satisfactory salaries, that some nonfinancial motivators were more effective than extra cash in building long-term employee engagement in most sectors, job functions, and business contexts. Many financial rewards mainly generate short-term boosts of energy, which can have damaging unintended consequences. When used poorly, monetary rewards can feel like coercion, an effect you see in the classic carrot-and-stick approach to motivation. According to leading researcher Edward Deci,

> *"Unless you're extremely careful with how you use rewards, you get people who are just working for the money. We need to compensate people fairly, but when we try to use money to motivate them to do tasks, it can very likely backfire on us."* {Endnote 30}

This becomes apparent when dealing with workers in an information economy. According to the Center for Talent Innovation (CTI), {Endnote 31} money is not the major motivator among college-educated workers. Today's employees are looking beyond conventional monetary rewards. And it doesn't take a huge budget. Many of these rewards can be free. Sylvia Ann Hewlett cites the results of a survey on working remotely, "83% of Millennials and 75% of Boomers say that the freedom to choose when and where they work motivates them to give 110%." {HBR Endnote 32}

TAKEAWAY: Look beyond dollars. Little things can make a big difference.

Chapter 4

A LITTLE SOMETHING EXTRA

"We picked up one excellent word –
a word worth traveling to New Orleans to get;
a nice, limber, expressive, handy word - lagniappe"

- Mark Twain

WHAT IF . . .

What if there was a simple marketing concept that moves the needle towards achieving differentiation, driving retention, reinforcing culture and stimulating word of mouth? What if your execution was 100% targeted, with zero waste and a personalized touch?

What is Lagniappe? Lagniappe is a creole word meaning *"the gift"* or *"to give more."* The practice originated in Louisiana in the 1840's whereby a merchant would give a little something extra. It is a signature personal touch by the business that creates goodwill and promotes word of mouth.

According to Webster's:

LAGNIAPPE (lan'yəp, lăn-yăp') *Chiefly Southern Louisiana & Mississippi* {Endnote 33}

1. A small gift presented by a storeowner to a customer with the customer's purchase.
2. An extra or unexpected gift or benefit. Also called regionally *boot.*

> *Etymology: Creole < French "la" + Spanish "ñapa."*
> *Interesting fact- Napa comes from yapa, which means*
> *"additional gift" in the South American Indian language,*
> *Quechua, from the verb yapay "to give more."*

ENTER SAMUEL LANGHORNE CLEMENS

According to Mark Twain in Life on the Mississippi:

> *We picked up one excellent word–a word worth traveling to New Orleans to get; a nice limber, expressive, handy word– "lagniappe."*

> *They pronounce it lanny-yap. It is Spanish–so they said. We discovered it at the head of a column of odds and ends in the [Times] Picayune [newspaper] the first day; heard twenty people use it the second; inquired what it meant the third; adopted it and got facility in swinging it the fourth.*

> *It has a restricted meaning, but I think the people spread it out a little when they choose. It is the equivalent of the thirteenth roll in a baker's dozen. It is something thrown in, gratis, for good measure.*

> *The custom originated in the Spanish quarter of the city. When a child or a servant buys something in a shop–or even the mayor or the governor, for aught I know–he finishes the operation by saying– 'Give me something for lagniappe.' The shopman always responds; gives the child a bit of licorice-root, gives the servant a cheap cigar or a spool of thread, gives the governor–I don't know what he gives the governor; support, likely.* {Endnote 34}

Employee **lagniappe**, i.e. green goldfish, is any time a business purposely goes above and beyond to provide a little something extra. It's a marketing investment in your employees.

It's that unexpected extra beyond compensation that is thrown in for good measure. Lagniappe helps drive differentiation, increase retention, promote word of mouth and reinforce corporate culture.

IS LAGNIAPPE JUST A BAKER'S DOZEN?

In order to understand a baker's dozen, we need to travel back to its origin in England. The concept dates back to the 13th century during the reign of Henry III. During this time there was a perceived need for regulations controlling quality, pricing and checking weights to avoid fraudulent activity. The Assize (Statute) of Bread and Ale was instituted to regulate the price, weight and quality of the bread and beer manufactured and sold in towns, villages and hamlets. {Endnote 35}

Bakers who were found to have shortchanged customers could be liable for severe punishment such as losing a hand with an axe. To guard against the punishment, the baker would give 13 for the price of 12, to be certain of not being known as a cheat.

The irony is that the statute deals with weight and not the quantity. The merchants created the "baker's dozen" to change perception. They understood that one of the 13 could be lost, eaten, burnt, or ruined in some way, leaving the customer with the original legal dozen.

A baker's dozen has become expected. Nowadays when we walk into a bakery and buy a dozen bagels, we expect the thirteenth on the house. Therefore it is not marketing lagniappe. Now if you provided a 14th bagel... that would be a green goldfish.

ACTS OF KINDNESS

Another way to think of employee lagniappe or green goldfish is as an act of kindness.

There are three "Acts of Kindness":

1. **Random Act of Kindness** - we've all seen this before. Good deeds or unexpected acts such as paying tolls, filling parking meters or buying gas. They are usually one-off, feel-

good activations. A random act of kindness draws upon gift economy principles. Giving with no expectation of immediate return.

2. **Branded Act of Kindness** – next level 2.0. Here the item given is usually tied closely with the brand and its positioning. It's less random, more planned and potentially a series of activations. This has the feel of a traditional marketing campaign.

3. **Lagniappe Act of Kindness** – 3.0 stuff. Kindness imbedded into your brand. Giving little unexpected extras (*g.l.u.e.*) as part of your DNA. This is rooted in the idea of "added value" to the transaction. Not a one off or a campaign, but an everyday practice that's focused on employees or customers. The beauty of creating green and purple goldfish is that there is no waste. Giving little extras to your current employees and customers. You are preaching to the choir... the folks who are already in church on Sunday.

THE NEED FOR INNOVATION AND TROJAN MICE

Everyone wants to go to heaven, but few are willing to pay the price. Actions speak louder than words when it comes to employee experience and building a strong culture. Brands need to start taking small steps to add value to the experience over time. Here is a great analysis by Peter Fryar on the concept of Trojan Mice: {Endnote 36}

> *Much change is of the "Trojan horse" variety. The planned changes are presented at a grand event (the Trojan Horse) amid much loud music, bright lights and dry ice. More often than not, however, a few weeks later the organization will have settled back into its usual ways and rejected much of the change. This is usually because the change was too great to be properly understood and owned by the workforce.*

Trojan mice, on the other hand, are small, well focused changes, which are introduced on an ongoing basis in an inconspicuous way. They are small enough to be understood and owned by all concerned but their effects can be far-reaching. Collectively a few Trojan mice will change more than one Trojan horse ever could.

TAKEAWAY: Employers are finding that supporting and incentivizing their staff improves motivation and engagement, which in turn impacts productivity. Take care of employees first with an inside out approach. Aim for increasing satisfaction and creating positive word of mouth. Your employees can become your best marketing asset.

Chapter 5

GIFT ECONOMY PRINCIPLES

*"There are two types of economies. In a commodity
(or exchange) economy, status is accorded to those who have the most.
In a gift economy, status is accorded to those who give the most to others."*

- Lewis Hyde

EXPLORING THE IDEAS OF SURPLUS AND STATUS

I'm fascinated by a concept of a "gift economy" and how it relates to culture. So – what is a gift economy?

According to Wikipedia:

> *"In the social sciences, a gift economy (or gift culture) is a society where valuable goods and services are regularly given without any explicit agreement for immediate or future rewards. Ideally, simultaneous or recurring giving serves to circulate and redistribute valuables within the community."* {Endnote 37}

A gift economy is the opposite of a market economy. In a market economy there is an exact exchange of values (*quid pro quo*). It is my belief that a hybrid called the lagniappe economy can sit between the two.

Can marketing lagniappe live in the middle? Here is a great analysis from a post by Kevin von Duuglass-ittu {Endnote 38} on gift economies:

> *This does not mean that the Gift Economy… and the Market Economy of business are incompatible, not in the least. In fact many if not most of our business exchanges are*

grounded in Gift-based relationships whose "gift" nature we simply are unconscious of and just assume. If you develop a keen eye for the gift-giving environment, and think about all of the things that gift-giving in those environments will signal, 1. a surplus others want to attach themselves to, 2. a magnanimous respect for the relationship beyond all else, 3. a debt structure that is positive.

Gift Economy

where valuable goods and services are regularly given without any explicit agreement for immediate or future rewards

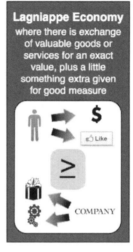

Lagniappe Economy

where there is exchange of valuable goods or services for an exact value, plus a little something extra given for good measure

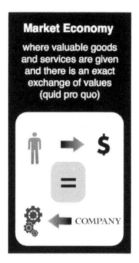

Market Economy

where valuable goods and services are given and there is an exact exchange of values (quid pro quo)

Let's examine each of the three through the lens of a lagniappe economy:

1. **Surplus** – the idea of surplus is grounded in giving extra or creating an inequality. Lagniappe comes from the Spanish "la napa" or the Quechan "yapay" both meaning "something that is added." Lagniappe is the practice by the business of giving little unexpected extras.

2. **Respect** – The gift or little extra is about the respect for the relationship. It becomes a beacon, a sign that shows you care. It's a physical sign of goodwill and employee appreciation.

3. **Positive** – A debt structure that is positive. This speaks to

exceeding expectations by giving extra. The idea of an equal exchange (market exchange) is a myth in marketing. You either exceed or fall short of expectations. Providing that extra value provides an inequality that is positive. The positive effect leads to a sort of indebtedness or reciprocity.

THE BENEFIT OF SURPLUS IS STATUS

As a business why would you want to incorporate gift economy principles into your culture? I believe there are three distinct reasons and corresponding benefits of the status gained through marketing lagniappe:

1. **Positioning** – stand out from your competition. If everyone is providing x, the fact that you provide x + y (gift) differentiates your offering. *Benefit: Differentiation*

2. **Loyalty** – giving the little extra (gift) enhances the employee experience. It creates a bond between the business and the employee. The benefit of that bond is increased loyalty as a form of repayment. *Benefit: Retention*

3. **Reciprocity** – Part of giving extra is to create goodwill (inequality). That inequality is repaid by positive word of mouth or digital word of mouse. The best form of marketing is via positive word of mouth. By giving signature extras, you provide something for your employees something to talk, tweet, Facebook, blog or post to Glassdoor about. *Benefit: Referrals*

PART II:

THE 5 INGREDIENTS OR
R.U.L.E.S. OF A GREEN GOLDFISH

Chapter 6

RELEVANCY

*"Take great care of your people, they'll take great
care of your customers, and your customers
will come back and back and back."*

- Bill Marriott Sr.

MAKING LAGNIAPPE IS LIKE MAKING JAMBALAYA

Have you ever made jambalaya? It's a bunch of different ingredients
all thrown in together. The chef takes a look at what's lying around
in the kitchen and throws it all into a pot. Let it stew with some
spices thrown in and voilà... you have yourself a jambalaya or a
green goldfish.

**Here are the five main ingredients or if you are an acronym fan
(like I am), the R.U.L.E.S:**

> **R**elevant – the item or benefit should be of value to your
> employees.
>
> **U**nexpected – the extra benefit or gift should leverage the
> benefit of surprise. It is something thrown in for good
> measure.
>
> **L**imited – if it's a small token or gift, try to select something
> that's rare, hard to find or unique to your business.
>
> **E**xpression – many times it comes down to the gesture. It
> becomes more about "how" it is given, as opposed to what is
> given.
>
> **S**tickiness – Is it memorable enough that the employee will
> want to share their experience by telling a friend or few
> hundred?

KEEPING IT RELEVANT

The first rule and probably the most important ingredient for a green goldfish is relevancy. If it's just a throw-in or SWAG (stuff we all get), it's probably not that relevant. A green goldfish needs to be something that is valued by your employees.

All the perks in the world won't make a difference if the overall culture doesn't include the most important factors. Among them: Do employees feel valued? Are there opportunities to grow? Do employees have good relationships with their managers?

Employers are finding that supporting and providing incentives for their staff improves motivation and engagement, which in turn impacts productivity. {Endnote 39}

Let's look at a handful of relevant examples from Clif Bar:

> #105 - The Emeryville-based nutrition company offers employees a half-hour of paid time to work out. Additionally, employees get 2.5 hours of free personal training per year.
>
> #106 - Environmental issues are very important to the company. Clif Bar gives their employees $6,500 toward the purchase of a fuel-efficient vehicle and $1,000 for an energy upgrade on their home.
>
> #139 – Clif Bar was born on a bike. The company gives employees $500 for the purchase of a commuter bike provided they agree to commute by bike at least twice per month.
>
> #872 - Employees receive a $350 stipend to help cover the entry costs for races, events and competitions.
>
> #874 - Every week the company assembles for a company

breakfast — bagels, fresh fruit, eggs, oatmeal, juice, bacon and sausage and more are served — and the team shares news, announcements and a consumer's letter of the week.

TAKEAWAY STAT: Clif Bar enjoys a retention rate of 96%.

Chapter 7

UNEXPECTEDNESS

"So what exactly is 'surprise and delight?'
It's when you give your customer something - that little
gift or 'extra mile' - that they didn't expect.
Surprise and delight is that small benevolent act that
shows that you put the customer first, and that
you're willing to make their experience special."

- Marc Schiller

WHAT IS A SCHEMA, ANYWAY?

Steve Knox wrote an article in Ad Age entitled, "Why Effective Word of Mouth Disrupts Schemas." {Endnote 40} The premise of the article is how you can leverage cognitive disruption to drive word of mouth. By doing something unexpected, you literally force people to talk about their experience.

First off, let me admit I had no clue what a "schema" was. So here is my interpretation of the word:

"It turns out that our brain remains typically in a static state. It relies on developing cognitive schemas to figure out how the world works. It recognizes patterns and adapts behavior accordingly. It basically doesn't want to have to think. For example, every day you get into the car and you know instinctively to drive on the right side of the road. Fast-forward and you're on a trip to the UK or Australia. The first time you drive on the left side it throws you for a loop. Its disruptive to your normal driving schema and it forces the brain to think, thereby it elicits discussion (i.e. word of mouth)."

Steve provided some great examples in his article, including a new brand of Secret deodorant from P&G. The deodorant utilized moisture activated ingredients that kicked in when you sweat. The brand understood that this could be positioned against a traditional schema, i.e. the more you workout, the more you sweat and the worse you smell. The counter-intuitive tagline for the brand became, "*The More You Move, the Better You Smell.*" Did it get people talking? A staggering 51,000 consumers posted comments on P&G's website about the product.

I started thinking how this idea of disruption applies to the concept of engagement and culture. The second ingredient in the R.U.L.E.S. is the concept of being **Unexpected**. It's that little something unexpected that triggers the disruption of our schemas.

Let's face it... most companies fail to deliver an exceptional employee experience. It's only when a brand goes above and beyond that we get shocked. And what happens when we receive that unexpected lagniappe act of kindness? We tell our friends, we tweet it and we post to Facebook about it.

Brazilian manufacturer Semco has a whole school of unexpected green goldfish. {Endnote 41} Here are some examples:

> #341 - All employees, including union members, have full access to all financials. Access is one thing, understanding is another. To educate its employees, Semco has created cartoons to help explain the financial data.

> #785 - Semco offers Up and Down Pay. For employees who are going through a phase in which they'd rather work less and lower their pay accordingly, the company does its best to adapt.

> #340 - Employees at Semco dictate their own salary. Twice a year they are given the chance to set their compensation structure.

#834 - Semco's employees have the flexibility to set their own hours.

#195 - Semco believes that it is important to meet people interested in working with the company, even if this interest is not immediate or there are no current opportunities. This led them to create the program – Date Semco. {Endnote 42} Good for prospective employees and current ones. Each gets a chance to meet in order to determine if the fit is right.

#462 - Employees are not allowed to sit in the same place two days in a row. This encourages collaboration and eliminates the need for managers to track time spent by employees at their desk.

TAKEAWAY STAT: Semco has had years where employee turnover has been as low as 1%.

Chapter 8

LIMITED

"America has believed that in differentiation, not in uniformity, lies the path of progress. It acted on this belief; it has advanced human happiness, and it has prospered."

- Louis Brandeis

SIGNATURE TOUCH

The third of the R.U.L.E.S. is the concept of being limited. What does limited mean? If it's a small token or extra, it means selecting something unique to your business. Ideally you want it to be signature to your brand. It is something rare, different or just plain hard to find elsewhere. A limited extra helps you to differentiate yourself in the marketplace, while providing insurance against being copied by competitors.

Etana is an insurance company in South Africa. The company is a market leader with a very open and unstructured culture. Etana has an interesting approach to culture. They believe in the importance of setting out values from the top, but that ultimately culture is what happens when you allow team members to do things. Empowerment, like a revolution (culture), starts from the bottom. Senior leadership at Etana lets employees (etanans) know that they don't need buy in. In the words of the Head of People & Culture, Carel Nolte, "Don't do what we say, do what is right." The company empowers etanans to take action and own the culture. Once they take initiative, Carel and the executive team step in with the necessary support.

Let's look at three signature examples from South Africa's Etana Insurance:

#925 - Etana is a Swahili word for "strong one." Employees [Etanans] tend to not take themselves seriously, but they take their business seriously. One team member lost a bet requiring him to run down a busy street in a speedo. In the spirit of having fun, senior leadership stepped in to raise the stakes. Employees were encouraged to join in for the run. Proceeds would go towards supporting a local men's charity. The daREDevil run is now an annual event with over 2,000 speedo-clad individuals running 4k (2.5 miles) to raise money for prostate and testicular cancer. {Endnote 43 }

#926 - Etana has an in house training department called the Etana Academy. {Endnote 44} The idea originated when a member of senior management came across an etanan tutoring a group of fellow etanans on a Saturday. Soon the idea of starting an accREDited learning facility was sprung. Etana now offers both online and offline courses serving etanans, their network members and even competitors.

#927 - The Etana REDwards applauds the efforts of those who have gone above and beyond in living the Etana values through their work. The event takes place during REDfast, a two-day getaway for all Etana staff. {Endnote 45} The awards are made by local artists and are given out to reinforce the core values at the company: **BE OPEN, KNOW, GROW, GIVE AND MAKE IT HAPPEN**. Here was a little extra that really drove home the recognition - to coincide with the event, Etana bought roadside billboards near the home office. The billboards highlighted the different winners from the REDwards. A total surprise and delight for employees when they returned to work.

Lesson from Etana: Engage employees and ignite their imaginations. Set your values and trust your employees to make the right decisions. A transformation from the ground up is more sustainable than from the top.

(Kurt Solomon – Winner of the "Make it Happen" REDward)

TAKEAWAY STAT: Over the last five years, Etana has seen revenues grow from 600 million rand to 2 billion. In 2012, Etana was voted Best Corporate Insurer at the 2012 Financial Intermediary Awards. {Endnote 46}

Chapter 9

EXPRESSION

"If you treat employees as if they make a difference to the company, they will make a difference to the company."

- Dr. James Goodnight

THE IMPORTANCE OF HOW

The fourth of the R.U.L.**E**.S. is expression. Expression speaks to *"how you give"* as opposed to *"what you give."* A green goldfish is a beacon. It's a sign that shows you care. That little extra touch demonstrates that your team members matter.

Let's look at a few examples from Nurse Next Door:

Nurse Next Door is a Canadian home healthcare provider. The company first showed up in the Purple Goldfish Project. {Endnote 47} They have an interesting way of handling mistakes with customers. And let's face it, we all make mistakes. It's how you handle them that makes the difference. In addition to sending a handwritten note, Nurse Next Door also sends a freshly baked apple pie to apologize. Literally, a humble pie.

Nurse Next Door has two unique green goldfish. The first is the *flowerbucks* program. As a core value-driven organization, team members demonstrating core values earn an in-house currency called *"Flowerbucks."* Each quarter the company holds *Flowerbuck Auctions* to celebrate core value award winners and auction off prizes ranging from gift cards to iPads and even trips.

The second program involves focusing employees' personal dreams. Nurse Next Door sits down with employees to uncover their goals. They've been able to support dreams ranging from learning to sail, to learning a new language, buying a home or even travelling.

Both of these programs converged recently to make one cool story. At a recent flowerbuck auction one of their employees won a trip because her co-workers gave her their flowerbucks. They did this because they learned her dream was to travel to South America and volunteer to teach English. All she needed was the airline ticket, so her coworkers donated their own flowerbucks. A great example of Paying it Forward. {Endnote 48}

Chapter 10

STICKINESS

"Why wait to be memorable?"

-Tony Robbins

STICKING OUT IN A SEA OF SAMENESS

The fifth of the R.U.L.E.**S**. is sticky. You want something that sticks. A strong marketing lagniappe promotes word of mouth. Your green goldfish needs to be memorable and talk-able.

Two questions to ask yourself:

1. Is it water cooler material both at the office and online?
2. Will your employees want to tell three people or 3,000?

Let's look at a sticky example from Peppercomm:

About six years ago, Steve Cody, one of **Peppercomm's** (#846) founders and a managing partner, started taking stand-up comedy classes for fun. He worked with Clayton Fletcher, {Endnote 49} a touring stand-up comedian, to build his chops.

> *"As he started doing more and more stand-up, he started to recognize that, although he was very good at client meetings and presentations, he was getting a lot better," says Deborah Brown, Partner and Managing Director, Strategic Development.* {Ragan.com Endnote 50}

Brown credits the training with developing not only speaking skills, but listening as well. It wasn't long before the entire management committee at Peppercomm was taking comedy training. It was sprung onto the team at an offsite meeting. Soon after that, everyone in the company was involved. "For the past five years, it's become part of our DNA," Brown says. Clayton Fletcher is now the Chief Comedy Officer at Peppercomm.

In fact, comedy training is now mandatory at the agency and part of the onboarding process. The training consists of learning about the different types of comedy such as observational humor. It's become a great way to meet the new hires with graduation consisting of a five minute set of stand-up. The agency has created fundraisers out of the performances as well as incorporating them into agency offsite meetings.

The training has become an integral part of Peppercomm. Deb Brown credits it with improving productivity, building teamwork and injecting fun into the agency. Humor is now part of the fabric of Peppercomm, whether it takes the form of spicing up an interoffice e-mail or creating a funny video for a client pitch. The agency has received a number of positive stories in the press and has recently started to extend the training to existing and prospective clients.

This whole approach of taking the business seriously, but not yourself, can be summed up in one quote from the agency:

> "Comedy training does more than create a unique culture. It produces a better business executive, someone who is just a tad ahead of their peers when it comes to listening skills, building audience rapport, and thinking in a nanosecond. Happy, funny employees are also the reason why we maintain so many long-term client relationships, experience low turnover, and produce amazing creativity. And that's no joke." {Endnote 51}

TAKEAWAY STAT: GETTING THE LAST LAUGH

The biggest benefactor of the comedy training has been the impact on culture at Peppercomm. The agency was recognized by Crain's as one to the Top 50 places to work in New York City. {Endnote 52} In case you are interested, here are the Top 5 in descending order:

5) Microsoft

4) Conductor

3) Allison + Partners

2) Squarespace

Drumroll please... 1) Peppercomm

PART III:

THE 15 TYPES OF GREEN GOLDFISH

Chapter 11

BASICS, BUILDING AND BELONGING

"There are no traffic jams along the extra mile."

- Roger Staubach

WHERE IS THE LOVE?

Motivation for employees is sagging. Recent reports show that motivation has fallen off at more that half of all companies. In difficult economic times, how can companies boost employee morale and drive high performance?

The simple answer is doing the little extras beyond compensation to demonstrate commitment to your employees. The Green Goldfish Project took a look at how companies go above and beyond to create signature extras. In examining the 1,001 examples of employee lagniappe, a few key themes emerged. Specifically, the different types of green goldfish can be categorized as the Three **B**'s:

(Photo Credit - Anita Ritenour Endnote 53)

1. **B**asics - Creating a stable environment where people can thrive

2. **B**elonging - Enabling high functioning teams and recognizing their efforts

3. **B**uilding - Empowering employees to learn, give back and take control of their destiny

CARING AND DOING THE RIGHT THING

Google sets the gold standard for taking care of its employees. No stone is left unturned in their quest to provide a welcoming and happy work environment. WHY? Here's an answer according to Google's Chief People Officer Laszlo Bock,

> *"It turns out that the reason we're doing these things for employees is not because it's important to the business, but simply because it's the right thing to do. And from a company standpoint, that makes it better to care than not to care."* {Endnote 54}

But there may be a more important reason according to Shawn Achor, CEO and Founder of Good Think,

> *"These aren't just PR Gimmicks. Smart companies cultivate these kinds of working environments; because every time an employee experiences a small burst of happiness, they get primed for creativity and innovation. They see solutions they might otherwise have missed." (Source: The Happiness Advantage)* {Endnote 55}

Google holds the top spot in the **Green Goldfish Project** {Endnote 56} with 20 entries. Let's have a look at a baker's dozen of their examples on the 9 inch journey:

FIRST INCH – ONBOARDING AND FOOD & BEVERAGE

#911 - **Breakfast, Lunch, Dinner and the Google 15.** One of the most cited perks of working at Google is the food. Google feeds its employees well. If you work at the Googleplex, you can eat breakfast, lunch and dinner free of charge. There are several cafés located throughout the campus, and employees can eat at any of them. The main café is Charlie's Place. The café takes its name from Google's first lead chef, Charlie Ayers. Before creating meals for Googlers, Ayers was the chef for the Grateful Dead. Although Ayers left Google in 2005, the café still bears his name. The café has several stations, each offering different kinds of cuisine. Options range from vegetarian dishes to sushi to ethnic foods from around the world. Google's culture promotes the use of fresh, organic foods and healthy meals. But when everything is free and you can eat whenever you want, it's easy to go overboard. That's where the Google 15 comes in. It refers to the 15 pounds many new Google employees put on once they start taking advantage of all the meals and snacks. Other cafés at the Googleplex include the Pacific Café, Charleston Café, Café 150 and the No Name Café. {Endnote 57}

SECOND INCH – SHELTER AND TRANSPARENCY

#191 - **The Lamborghini of toilets.** Googlers have access to some of the most high-tech toilets around. These Japanese johns offer washing and drying of your nether regions as well as the mysterious "wand cleaning." Both the wash water and the seat itself can be warmed or cooled depending on your preference. {Huffington Post Endnote 58}

THIRD INCH – WELLNESS, TIME AWAY & MODERN FAMILY

#179 - Google is giving its employees in same-sex relationships extra cash to cover their partners' health benefits. Currently, when receiving partner health care coverage, same-sex domestic partners are subject to an extra tax that traditional, married couples aren't required to pay. Google is taking the burden of paying this tax on itself by compensating partnered LGBT employees for the amount of the tax, which comes to a bit more than $1,000 each year. This benefit will also cover any dependents of the partner in the same-sex couple. {Mashable Endnote 60}

#691 – One perk about **not** working at Google is that [the website] Gawker never posts a photo of you swimming in one of the Googleplex's lap pools. The outdoor mini-pools are like water treadmills: a strong current allows employees to swim and swim and go nowhere. Luckily, according to How Stuff Works, lifeguards are always on duty in case someone gets in over their head. {Huffington Post **Endnote 59**}

FOURTH INCH – RETIREMENT AND FLEXIBILITY

#40 - Taken from a post by Meghan Casserly in Forbes, "In a rare interview with Chief People Officer Laszlo Bock I discovered that the latest perk for Googlers extends into the afterlife. 'This might sound ridiculous,' Bock told me recently in a conversation on the ever-evolving benefits at Google, 'But we've announced death benefits at Google.' Should a U.S. Googler pass away while under the employ of the search giant, their surviving spouse or domestic partner will receive a check for 50% of their salary every year for the next decade. Even more surprising, a Google spokesperson confirms that there's 'no tenure requirement' for this benefit, meaning most of their 34,000 Google employees qualify." {Forbes Endnote 61}

#343 - Former Google Executive Marissa Mayer [now Yahoo! CEO and telecommuting killer] believes women are especially susceptible to burning out because they are faced with more demands in the home. "What causes burnout, Mayer believes, is not working too hard," Rosin writes. "People, she believes, 'can work arbitrarily hard for an arbitrary amount of time,' but they will become resentful if work makes them miss things that are really important to them." She gave an anecdote for how she kept one Google executive, whom she calls "Katy," from quitting. Katy loved her job and she loved her team and she didn't mind staying late to help out. What was bothering Katy was something entirely different. Often, Katy confessed, she showed up late at her children's events because a meeting went overly long, for no important reason other than meetings tend to go long. And she hated having her children watch her walk in late. For Mayer, this was a no-brainer. She instituted a Katy-tailored rule. If Katy had told her earlier that she had to leave at four to get to a soccer game, then Mayer would make sure Katy could leave at four. Even if there was only five minutes left to a meeting, even if Google co-founder Sergey Brin himself was mid sentence and expecting an answer from Katy, Mayer would say "Katy's gotta go" and Katy would walk out the door and answer the questions later by e-mail after the kids were in bed." The key to sustaining loyalty in employees is making sure they get to do the things that are most important to them outside of work. {Business Insider **Endnote 62**}

FIFTH INCH – TEAM BUILDING AND COLLABORATION

#205 - Google knows how to roll. It has a bowling alley for employees.

#692 - Google's Conference Bike is used as a team-building exercise for new employees. It has four wheels and five riders who work together to move it around. {PC Magazine Endnote 63}

#892 - One of things shaping culture at the search leader are "TGIF" meetings. They tend to happen most Fridays, said Craig Silverstein, who joined the founders as Google's first employee in 1998. TGIF, where any Googler is free to ask the founders any company-related question, became a fixture of the culture. {Mercury News Endnote 64}

SIXTH INCH – ATTABOYS AND ATTAGIRLS

#941 - The Founders' Award, Google's most significant and high profile recognition program, is designed to give extraordinary rewards for extraordinary team accomplishments. While there's no single yardstick for measuring achievement, a general rule of thumb is that the team being rewarded has accomplished something that created tremendous value for Google. The awards pay out in the form of Google Stock Units (GSUs) that vest over time. Team members receive awards based on their level of involvement and contribution, and the largest awards to individuals can reach several million dollars. In 2005, Google awarded approximately $45 million in restricted stock to employees working on 11 different projects. {Great Places to Work Endnote 65}

SEVENTH INCH – TRAINING AND DEVELOPMENT

#543 - Google's "CAREERGURU" program matches Google executives with Google employees to provide confidential, one-on-one career coaching and guidance around the subjects of work-life balance, personal and professional development, communication styles, and conflict resolution, among others. {Business Insider Endnote 66}

EIGHTH INCH – GIVING BACK AND PAYING IT FORWARD

#912 - Google Outreach. Google teams up with charitable organizations and NGO's to leverage Google Earth to promote their causes.

#2 – According to Jonathan Strickland in HowStuffWorks: How the Googleplex Works, {Endnote 67} the company allows its employees to use up to 20% of their week at Google to pursue special projects. That means for every standard work-week, employees can take a full day to work on a project unrelated to their normal workload. Many of Google's products (i.e. Gmail and Google News) started out as pet projects in the 20% time program.

#36 - The Google-O-Meter {Endnote 68} gives all employees a voice on employee suggestions and potential cultural changes. Google's Chief Culture Officer Stacy Sullivan implemented the company's charting tool, the Google-O-Meter, to gauge the popularity of employee suggestions, such as housing more doctors on site or bringing overseas employees to headquarters for a visit. "It wasn't something that we would just go and implement for them," she says. "Their suggestions had to be reflective of things about the culture that [many] people wanted to change." {Entrepreneur Endnote 69}

Chapter 12

RECRUITING, ONBOARDING AND F&B

*"We don't know where our first impressions
come from or precisely what they mean,
so we don't always appreciate their fragility."*

- Malcolm Gladwell, Author of *The Tipping Point*

The next three chapters cover the types of green goldfish associated with "**BASICS**":

Attitudes begin to form at the initial point of contact with an organization. There is no better place to start applying G.L.U.E. {Endnote 70} than when you are welcoming new employees to your company. Smart companies take advantage of these early days in order to ensure a strong, productive, and dedicated workforce.

> *"The way you manage the transition of somebody into your culture speaks volumes about the culture to the person coming in, because you're making those first early impressions and they know what's expected of them"* says George Bradt, Managing Director at PrimeGenesis. {Inc.com Endnote 71}

ONBOARDING

The formal transition process for new employees is called onboarding. Here's how it is defined:

> *Onboarding, also known as organizational socialization, refers to the mechanism through which new employees acquire the necessary knowledge, skills, and behaviors to become effective organizational members and insiders.*

Tactics used in this process include formal meetings, lectures, videos, printed materials, or computer-based orientations to introduce newcomers to their new jobs and organizations. {Wikipedia Endnote 72}

Unfortunately less than 25% of organizations have a formal onboarding process. According to onboarding pioneer and expert George Bradt,

"Most organizations haven't thought things through in advance. On their first day, they are welcomed by such confidence building remarks as: Oh, you're here... we'd better find you an office." {Endnote 73}

WHY ONBOARDING?

Research shows that employees make the critical decision to stay or leave within the first six months. New hires that participate in an onboarding program can "maximize retention, engagement, and productivity." {HCI White Paper Endnote 74} Socialization efforts lead to positive outcomes for new employees, including higher job satisfaction, better job performance, greater organizational commitment and reduction in stress.

Yet, culturally onboarding new hires can be a real challenge. While sleek videos, laminated pocket cards and lobby placards may help employees memorize company values, the actual understanding of how to "live" the company values can be a whole other story. Your culture is only as cohesive as the people willing to live out the shared values. Once again, actions speak louder than words.

Having a diverse range of ways to welcome a new hire is critical to establishing a healthy employer-employee relationship. Here are a baker's dozen of companies that purposefully go the extra mile to engage new team members:

Welcome Wagon

JM Smucker (#575) new hires get a gift basket sent to their homes. {Business Insider Endnote 75}

Intel's (#534) new hires have dedicated greeters and gifts waiting for them when they arrive on their first days as a part of their hands-on new employee orientation. {Business Insider Endnote 76)

Online glasses manufacturer **Warby Parker** (#171) gives a welcome package to new employees. The package includes the founder's favorite pretzels and a gift certificate to a Thai restaurant, since the founders lived off Thai food during their startup phase. {New York Times Endnote 77}

BUDDIES AND CUSTOMIZATION

Sweet workspaces. **Asana** (#143) gives each employee $10,000 to spend on their office setup. The most common choice is a sweet motorized desk that allows a person to sit or stand by just hitting a button (because we all know standup desks can save your life).

The workspace customization is just one step in the onboarding process at Asana. The company outlines 5 steps in a **recent post**. Here they are summarized:

1. **Minimize Chores** – they set up their desk and computer in advance and provide $10K for further customization.
2. **Assign a Buddy** – A co-worker with tenure gets assigned to the new developer.
3. **Adding Value on Day One** – new employees **must** ship [deliver] something on Day One. It could be a tiny product improvement, or a fix to a bug or a typo—anything.
4. **Meet the Team** - The buddy schedules a series of learning sessions on various engineering topics over the first few weeks.

5. **Starter Project** - Each new hire gets the same starter project: to build a small chat application. {Endnote 78}

Capital One (#361) runs a *Buddy Assimilation Program*. The program matches veterans with newcomers. "Buddies" like show the newbies around, have lunch with them and act as a resource. After a month of training, new employees work "in the nest" for two weeks, fielding incoming calls with plenty of support. Hands go up whenever a trainee has a question, and a roving supervisor runs over to help. Once on their own, employees work within teams. But they're never far from a helping hand as team leaders and "floor walkers" decked in bright red and yellow vests are always available to answer questions. {Tampa Bay Tribune Endnote 79}

Every associate at ladder(less) **W. L. Gore & Associates** (#539) has a sponsor who coaches, mentors, and commits to helping that person succeed at the company. {Business Insider Endnote 80}

UNDERSTANDING THE BUSINESS

USAA (#456) figuratively runs a Boot Camp. The insurance provider for military members and their families has an interesting onboarding process for new employees. Training includes trying on military fatigues, eating MRE's (ready to eat meals) and reading letters from family members. {Jeanne Bliss Endnote 81}

Exposure makes a difference in performance. According to {Fast Company Endnote 82} that's the finding of Adam Grant, a Wharton professor who studied the training given to 71 new call center employees of a mid-western software firm:

> One group of trainees was chosen to meet an 'internal customer'-- an employee of another department whose salary depends on the sales that the new hires make--during their initial training. In combination with some inspirational

words from the CEO, this contact with a real live beneficiary significantly improved both sales and revenue during the employees' first seven weeks. The difference? A not-insignificant 20% improvement in revenue per shift. Leadership messages from the CEO about purpose, vision, mission, and meaning, however, had no such effect on their own.

WRITING THE SHIP

According to Harvard Professor and noted author Teresa Amabile, {Endnote 83} the ability to track small wins can help to motivate big accomplishments. Rituals like writing in a diary can be a strong influencer. The number one driver for inner work-life is making progress on meaningful work. Reflection can become an important part of the process.

New hires at custom t-shirt company **CustomInk** (#514) receive a blank journal. They are encouraged to record any interesting things they learn about the company in their notebook during their orientation or any questions they would like to ask. New hires are also asked to record instances where they've seen CustomInk's values in action. At the 30-day mark, new hires convene to share what they've noted in their journals. Making new hires accountable for noticing how their colleagues and managers live those values every day helps brings those behaviors to life. {Great Places to Work Endnote 84}

PICTURE THIS

Hulu (#918) has an interesting approach to reinforce culture. The company encourages employees [hulugans] to bring their passions to work and has an interesting way of showing it during the onboarding process:

In the words of John Foster, Hulu's Head of Talent and Organization,

"When you enter our office, the first thing you notice is a wall of portraits with every team member showing off a bit of his or her personality. From this gigantic photo wall, even a casual visitor will quickly notice that our people are our most precious asset." {Endnote 85}

Hulu hires a professional photographer to shoot all new hires. The only direction by Hulu is to bring whatever you are passionate about. The pictures are then placed in the lobby for all to see. Over 700 portraits adorn the wall.

GAMIFY

New employees at **Snagajob** (#703) are asked to share their unique talents and experiences in a brief questionnaire. The answers are shared among employees over the company's employee-only online network. When new hires [snaggers] are introduced at weekly company-wide meetings, employees are quizzed about the responses and get token rewards such as candy for each correct answer. "It's a fun way to hold our employees accountable for learning about our new snaggers," says Betsy Kersey, whose title at Snagajob is Director of People. {Entreprenuer.com Endnote 86}

RETURNSHIPS

TD Bank (#489) worked with the University of Toronto's Rotman School of Management to develop the Rotman Back to Work program for women who have been out of the workforce for over eight years -- and operates the in-house "Back to Business" rotational work program for women returning to work. {Endnote 87}

CHECK-INS

When employees join **Davies PR** (#723), they are given a 3-month, 6-month, 9-month and annual review to ensure they get a "Best Start" at Davies. After one year at the company, employees receive annual 360-degree reviews in which they are assessed by their co-workers. {PR News Online Endnote 88}

TECHNOLOGY SPURRING DIALOGUE

Companies are using new tools and procedures to assimilate its latest hires. **Veson Nautical** (#827), a Boston-based software developer for risk management for the maritime industry, just instituted a new program in January called *FastStart*, an online tool from consulting firm Blessing White that aligns work styles and priorities between new employees and managers. "The manager ranks the skills important and less important to the job, and the employee does the same," says Sarah Taffee, director of human resources and organization effectiveness at Veson Nautical. "The employee has the opportunity to compare their own answers with their manager's answers, and then the system guides them through how to have an open discussion about those things." {Inc.com Endnote 89}

FINDING YOUR WAY

Box.net (#825) gives entry level employees three months to explore all the different departments of the company and you train them so that they know your products and services backward and forward— and then you allow the employee to choose what department they feel is the best fit for them. {Inc.com Endnote 90}

PUTTING CULTURE ON THE FIRING LINE

The offer is part of the four-week new hire paid training at Zappos. The training immerses the group into the culture and Zappos' laser focus on customer service. At the conclusion of training, everyone is offered a packet of cash to leave. The amount has been raised numerous times over the years and now the current offer is $3,000.

According to Fast Company Co-Founder Bill Taylor in HBR,

"It's a small practice with big implications: Companies don't engage emotionally with their customers – people do. If you want to create a memorable company, you have to fill your company with memorable people. How are you making sure that you're filling your organization with the right people? And how much are you willing to pay to find out?" {Endnote 91}

Zappos challenges employees to fully commit to the company. Are you making a bold statement to reinforce your corporate culture?

TAKEAWAY STAT: In case you're keeping score at home, roughly 2-3% of trainees at Zappos have taken the offer since it was rolled out. {Endnote 92}

Food & Beverage

"When employees go home to their working-class neighborhoods,
they compare jobs. One of our employees might say,
'I get a free, hot meal every day,'
and his neighbor says, 'Really? I have to brown-bag it.'
That is what I think of as WOMP -- word-of-mouth potential –
and it works as well in hiring as it does in marketing."

- Mike Jannini, Former Senior Executive, Marriott

Little things can make a big difference. Even silly little things like M&M'S. Food and beverage is part of the Basics, the first steps towards improving employee engagement. For a shining example, we head to the world's largest privately held software company.

Recognizing employees for their value to the company was part of the early SAS Institute's heritage. People who worked for the company during its earliest days on Hillsborough Street (across from NC State) tell stories of piling into Dr. Jim Goodnight's station wagon and going down the street for pizza (#437). SAS would pick up the tab whenever the company added another 100 customer sites to the list. A flexible work environment and some of the trademarks or beacons of the employee-friendly SAS culture, including M&M'S and breakfast goodies, were born in the first months of the company's existence. {SAS Institute Endnote 93}

HOUSTON, WE HAVE A PROBLEM

The culture of the SAS Institute was formed out of direct experiences of its founder, Dr. James Goodnight. According to a case study by The Wharton School,

> Before founding SAS Institute, Goodnight worked briefly at NASA. What he found there was an environment in which people did not communicate. Any effort to build trust was absent: NASA used timecards to make sure that employees

worked their full allotment of hours, and there were metal detectors to ensure that employees weren't stealing. That wasn't all. At NASA, executives were supposed to be seen as "different" from the rest of the workers. There were special executive parking areas. Executives had their own break and dining area, with free, "good" coffee. Everyone else had to dump a quarter into a vending machine if they wanted coffee or a soft drink. Goodnight decided that when he started his own company, he would create a very different environment. {Endnote 94}

From the outset Goodnight worked towards creating a fun place to work (#48), with the work itself being the biggest reward. An environment that would harness creativity, providing all of the resources employees would need. Simply living by the golden rule and treating people the way he would like to be treated. The entire approach can be summed up by an employee's quote in Fast Company,

> *"You're given the freedom, the flexibility, and the resources to do your job. Because you're treated well, you treat the company well."* {Endnote 95}

GOOD BUSINESS

At a time when annual turnover in some information technology shops is as high as 30% and filling empty positions can cost anywhere from two to five times an employee's salary, IT firms are discovering what SAS Institute has known for decades. That it takes more than just a paycheck to keep their people happy. In the SAS Institute view, money should not be the key motivator. People that care primarily about the money can easily be bought. It's simple according to Dr. Goodnight,

> *"You have two choices. You can spend money on employees or headhunters and training, and it's about the same amount of money. So why not spend it on the employees?"* {Endnote 96}

Is it working? SAS Institute has never had a single layoff in its entire history. It has less than 3% mean turnover, year over year growth and a focus on long-term growth rather than satisfying shareholders' immediate requirements.

TAKEAWAY STAT: SAS averages 4,000 resumes for every job opening.

FREE FOR ALL

All of the benefits and perks are available to all employees, and everyone on campus is a SAS Institute employee, including software engineers, salespeople, childcare workers and groundskeepers. Founder Goodnight strongly believes that people are much more committed if they are part of the company. All employees have the same exact bonus plan potential.

Here are some of the Good Eats examples at SAS:

#437 - Free fresh fruit every Monday, M&M'S on Wednesday, Breakfast goodies every Friday and Break rooms stocked with complimentary soft drinks, juices, crackers, coffee / tea.

#942 - Employee events and celebrations, including the annual family picnic, the elegant winter party and end-of-the-month parties.

#436 - *Coffee with Goodnight.* Once a month employees can sign up to sit down with SAS founder Dr. G for some coffee and biscuits (Goodnight has a supposed weakness for Biscuitville.) Eight to 10 employees get randomly selected for the hour-long session. The first 15 minutes are an update on the state of the company by Goodnight with the remainder open for employee questions. No topics are off limits.

#832 – A piano player plays at lunch in one of the SAS campus cafeterias three days a week. Meals are relatively cheap and an emphasis is put on healthy food for employees. {Inc Endnote 97}

#943 - Sushi chef, Namjoon Kim is one of three chefs who prepare made to order sushi rolls at lunch in the newest SAS employee cafeteria. {Inc Endnote 98}

Let's look at Baker's Dozen of companies that provide signature Food & Beverage extras:

FBNA is an acronym for "Free Beer, No A--holes." It is the pseudo tagline {Endnote 99} for marketing agency **Ryan Partnership** and an unofficial mantra for many others. Some like the Australian software company **Atlassian** make it a hiring requirement. The company has a recipe for selecting potential hires called the "beer test" according to co-founder Mike Cannon-Brookes, "I ask myself would I find it interesting to have a beer with this job applicant?" {Endnote 100}

Let's bring on a six-pack of beer and wine examples:

Beer O'Clock

At **Cirrus Logic** (#58) weekly happy hours encourage engineers to interact and share ideas. The company also sponsors guitar lessons, on-site yoga, and photography courses. Every month, the company hosts "Cirrus Logic Rocks!"—a live music event featuring local musicians—on its outdoor patio. {greatplacetowork.com Endnote 101}

It's the tasty perk everyone wants, but few provide: *Free Beer*. Cold brew is always on tap at **HubSpot's** (#135) headquarters in Cambridge, MA where the kitchen has a designated beer fridge stocked with at least 50 different brands. "We have Stella, Beck's, Guinness, Bud Light," said Kara Sassone, the company's media relations specialist, as she rattles off the more popular labels. A cold one helps to encourage employees to hang out at the office and build better working relationships, the company says.

Free or not, beer -- as with all good things -- is best in moderation, especially at the office. Even so, it's a popular perk. "I'm sure if we were to get rid of the beer fridge here at HubSpot, the whole company would be up in arms," blogged one employee. {boston.com Endnote 102}

DPR Construction (#75) and its Wine Bars. You can drink Merlot in all 17 of the Redwood City, Calif.-based company's offices, except for its Austin location, which has a saloon with beer on tap. {Fiscal Times Endnote 103}

You can't mess with Beer Fridays. **F5 Networks** (#119), once a scrappy Seattle startup and now a major provider of IT infrastructures, has once again left its competition in the dust with a refreshing, hoppy, end-of-the-week tradition that has lasted since its early days. "Beer Friday," one employee tells us, "is core to the culture of F5." Even those who don't drink are fans of Beer Friday, which they refer to as "Free peanuts, chips and veggies Friday." Refreshments aside, in an office of more than 750 people, (and 2,000 around the globe) they also just appreciate the chance for a weekly get-together with co-workers from other departments. {NWJobs.com Endnote 103}

Grabbing a shot from the Jägermeister machine in the Z Bar, showing off their karaoke chops, getting uber-comfy in the Nightlight oom--no, people aren't visiting Belltown's newest hot spot. It's Seattle agency **Zaaz** (#121), a 150-person Web design, analytics and optimization firm. {NWJobs.com Endnote 104}

Grasshopper.com (#797) has a unique set of wheels. According to Ambassador of Buzz Taylor Aldredge,

> *"Our beer cart is a motorized cooler that can be driven around the office. Also, it comes with a caboose for more storage. We've used it for things like Beer Fridays, or to*

transport supplies to cookouts outside. Also, we've used it to introduce new employees around the office by having them sit on the caboose as someone drove them around. It's a great multi-purpose vehicle."

THE OTHER BREW

While there's a lot of good coffee in San Francisco, Blue Bottle is among the best. It's also kind of expensive. But luckily for **Zynga** employees, you can get free coffee from Blue Bottle at Zynga's "dog house" headquarters (#148) in San Francisco. {BusinessInsider.com Endnote 105}

Jetsetter (#174) maintains a tab at the local coffee shop, so teammates don't have to eat the cost of networking while working.

The headquarters for **Sophos** (#648) is located in an old bank branch office. The renovated head office features a 24/7 lounge complete with video games, foosball, billiards and a self-serve lunch room with free coffee / tea.

IT'S JUST LUNCH

"We try to stay frugal — our office furniture is secondhand, but we cater lunch in at ZocDoc (#138) everyday," says Allison Braley of ZocDoc. "We've tried to be really thoughtful about the perks we offer — lunch helps people get to know ZocDoc-ers from other departments. Aeron chairs don't." {Mashable Endnote 106}

Submitted by Taylor Aldredge, "I'm the Ambassador of Buzz at Grasshopper (#774), a virtual phone system for entrepreneurs. We have a Wii and/or Playstation 3 room, free healthy food and drinks all day, a pool table, and a green lunch program that gives people $5 a day towards their lunch." The $5 towards lunch stood out, so I asked Taylor how that worked. "The $5 Green Lunch is pretty straight-forward. Grasshopper provides $5/day through a house account at DiningIn.com. So, you can order food from one of the restaurants at a discount, and it all gets delivered to the office. This way nobody's driving for lunch, and you're saving money by getting lunch at $5 off."

PROVIDING HEALTHIER FOOD AND SNACKS

U.S. workers eat tons of sugary and fatty junk food, often because that's all they have time to scarf down between meetings. Though you can't be expected to single-handedly halt the U.S. culture's mad rush into obesity, companies can make it easier for workers to make better choices, whether its by making healthy foods more readily available or having a long enough lunch break so that fast food is only an option rather than a necessity.

From bins filled with free healthy snacks to tapping a keg at 4 p.m. every afternoon, **Digitas** (#162) offers employees a wide variety of perks and benefits to keep them energized. {ChicagoBusiness.com Endnote 107}

At **Morningstar** (#577), they believe that even "the little things count," which is why the company provides employees with an egalitarian environment, free beverages, free bagels on Wednesday and casual dress every day. {BusinessInsider.com Endnote 108}

Team members at **Realeflow** (#423) make daily smoothies. The ritual every so often turns into a fun competition where taste and nutrition are the criteria used to judge the winner. {Outside Magazine Endnote 109}

NYC PR Agency **Lippe Taylor** (#727) tries to offer employees the best of both worlds: financial benefits typically found only in big companies, and the hands-on touch of hominess and caring that comes with a smaller company. It feeds its employees early and often: from morning perk Mondays (breakfast spread of bagels, muffins, fresh fruit, orange juice), to its signature Sweet Treat on Wednesdays. Creativity abounds with account executives pairing seasonal tie-ins with tasty treats—think mini milkshakes on National Milkshake Day and chips and salsa for Cinco de Mayo. {PR News Online Endnote 110}

DINNER IS SERVED

Take-home dinners are provided at **Genentech** (#438).

Employees at **Facebook** (#440) can take home a free dinner or, if working late, their families can come in to eat with them, leading to a regular sight of children in the campus cafeteria. {NY Times Endnote 111}

PAVLOV'S PAYDAY GOODNESS

Blue Buddha (#781), a maker of custom jewelry, provides employees with premium chocolate on paydays. The General Operations Manager purchases the chocolate ahead of time and then distributes two pieces to each person. Sometimes they'll pick up chocolate when they walk in and go past the manager's desk. Everyone has a physical "inbox" so for people who aren't there, the manager will put the chocolate in their inbox so it is there for them on their next working day. {Blue Buddha Endnote 112}

Chapter 13

SHELTER AND TRANSPARENCY

"It seems as if it was just a few years ago that we were taking people out of offices and putting them into cubicles. From there, the trend went to open work spaces, then hoteling, and then shared hoteling "cubes"—all driven by the need to keep real-estate costs low in a very acquisitions-oriented industry that's always streamlining. Now, more and more of our employees are working remotely. In many ways, that's a good thing. It gives people a lot more flexibility and freedom, and makes them happier about the job because they're able to put their lives together in ways that matter to them."

- Rebecca Ranninger, Chief HR Officer, Symantec

GIMME SHELTER

The second inch on the journey to driving employee engagement is Shelter. Pure and simple... Space Matters. It sets the stage for how you both work and interact on the job. Beyond functionality, the physical environment should be able to tell the story of the company. According to Mark Fidelman,

> *"The best workplaces find a way to integrate their organization's culture and mission. In the future, these workspaces will also help your workforce to become more effective. An adaptive workplace – where physical objectives and software adapt to the working style of the organization and not the other way around. Work in the workplace will become more human and more results oriented."* {Forbes.com Endnote 113}

TO CUBE OR NOT TO CUBE?

The word cube has four letters. The traditional view is that it's a bad four letter word. No one aspires to work in a cube. My sister in the early 90's worked at a benefits consulting practice in Philadelphia.

Positioned in an interior cube and bathed in florescent light, she would joke about the desire for an office. The senior team at the firm (all men) occupied them all. *"No balls, no walls"* was the inside joke.

Some workplaces mandate that there are no offices. Zappos, for example, is entirely a cube culture. Even the management team sits in an area affectionately dubbed as "Monkey Row." {Endnote 114} Other workplaces take the concept one step further. No offices or cubes, just rows of desks with no barriers like at the agency Gyro. {Endnote 115}

Maybe the answer is somewhere in between open and closed. Mary Lee Duff of Interior Architects {Endnote 116} chimes in,

> *"The traditional concept of the high panel Dilbert cubicle has definitely been diminishing. The drive today is for workplace settings to be more open and collaborative with a strong emphasis on flexibility. For some clients that means going into benching systems, for others it is simply lowering the panel walls and being able to offer greater control over how to reconfigure one's own space."*

MOVING FROM "I" TO "WE"

Flexibility is key, but so is diversity. Here is an interesting take by Steelcase CEO, Jim Hackett,

> *"Celebrate the shift of what we call the 'I' space to the 'we' space... Space has to enable and empower information in ways we only imagine... across a continuum of I and we work... people need a range of settings to accommodate focused, collaborative and social work in both open and enclosed environments – in other words, a palette of place."* {Forbe.com Endnote 117}

Let's have a look at a Baker's Dozen of companies who've tackled space (the "Final Frontier") with a little something extra:

OPEN AND FLEXIBLE BY DESIGN

Kayak.com (#64) has an open office environment. In the words of CTO Paul English, "I sit out with the product managers. We hold design meetings at one another's desks throughout the day. We do design interaction like that, where everyone can hear and anyone can jump in. If anyone needs to make a private phone call, there are a few private offices, but our general philosophy is that an open environment facilitates intellectual intensity. Most engineers are introverted. Here, when people overhear a discussion, we encourage them to walk over and say, 'There's another way to do that." {Inc.com Endnote 118}

In an effort to foster collaboration among the 15 employees at brand communications firm **Trevelino/Keller** (#241), there are no offices at the firm's HQ. The space at the King Plow Arts Center is open, both philosophically and physically. "There's no place to hide," says agency principal Dean Trevelino jokingly. Trevelino empowers his employees to make their own decisions to get the work done. "Everyone expects each other to work hard and do it with no ego." {Atlanta Business Chronicle Endnote 119}

David Clarke, **BGT Partners** (#737) co-founder and managing partner, purposefully designed the office to have an open feel with "huddle rooms" for staff to verbalize any issues or ideas. "So often, IMs or e-mails get misconstrued. We want to encourage people to come back and forth and explore all other areas of the company if they're interested. We can only tell you to do so much." {AdAge.com Endnote 120}

According to Jörg Pierach, **Fast Horse Inc.** (#296) founder and president, "We don't have offices, cubes or even assigned desks, which leads to greater collaboration while we're in the office, and allows people to be equally productive when they are away.

Employees have the opportunity to work from virtually anywhere they have an Internet connection on a regular basis. And, during the summer, our office is closed on Fridays, allowing people to work from home in the morning and then get a jump on their summer weekend in the afternoon." {Minneapolis / St. Paul Business Journal Endnote 121}

TD Bank (#448) has *FlexWorkPlace* pilot program to accommodate changing and flexible work patterns. It features redesigned floors that include more meeting rooms, no traditional offices, and a "collaborative" cafe where employees can meet and work in a comfortable and informal setting. {Endnote 122}

EAT, PRAY, WORK

According to some reports, the cost of stress in the workplace is approaching $300 billion per year in absenteeism, tardiness, poor performance, employee turnover, accidents, and stress-related workers' compensation claims. What's a brand to do?

The online marketplace **eBay** (#123) offers both prayer and meditation rooms. Employees can sit in silence—in minimalist rooms decorated in earth tones, accented with cushy pillows, floor mats and fragrant flower buds—to catch a few critical moments of solitude and to decompress from the myriad stresses of a workday. {cult-branding.com Endnote 123}

No one at **PARTNERS + simons** (#131) has to leave the office to make a private phone call. Instead, they slip inside one of two large, soundproof tubes in the company's coffee and kitchen area where they can chat away. The South Boston ad agency has two cellphone booths that look like something out of the transporter room from "Star Trek." Trudy Almquist, CFO at the agency, said that employees were regularly using conference and meetings room for private calls to their spouses or their children's schools. "Conference room time was at a premium, and this was a better option," she said,

> *"It's just a place to talk to your doctor, your spouse, or whatever you have going on in your life. It's to have a little privacy in a public place."* {boston.com Endnote 124}

Forget hours of toiling under harsh lights, in a stiff chair or trapped in a maze of confined spaces. At **Alberici's** (#323) headquarters, the light pours in through walls of windows, the chairs are ergonomically designed to draw out body heat, and the space is so open and sleek that it feels as if a library and modern art gallery hooked up. "It's a little overwhelming when you walk in," says project engineer Peter Nuernberger. A native prairie and white wind turbine outside offer a preview of the building's environmentally friendly design. Inside, bamboo covers elevator walls, and employees dine on heart-healthy subsidized lunches. Everything whispers of the company's innovative culture—with an emphasis on whispers. In fact, the company even plays white noise throughout the day. "It is kind of like working in a library," says Jay Reiter, Director of Marketing. {St. Louis Business Journal Endnote 125}

Shhh... **SAP Canada's** (#450) headquarters offers a quiet room for employees who need a quick break during the busy day.

WORKING TOWARDS HOME

The professional services recruitment firm **Goodman Masson** (#335) doesn't just want to make a stable home for its employees — it wants to help them buy one too or pay off an existing mortgage. If the London-based financial services recruitment firm's 135 workers save 20% of basic pay for three years their employer will add 33% to that deposit/lump sum saving — or 50% if they add bonuses too. {The Sunday Times Endnote 126}

Employees of **Paramount Staffing** (#548) purchasing a home for the first time receive $5,000. {Business Insider Endnote 127}

KITCHEN CONFIDENTIAL

At **Clockwork Active Media Systems** (#289) the best gathering of the day is the one that takes place every single morning. Clockwork has a large kitchen table that seats about 25 people. Every morning the table is packed with employees starting their day with a cup of coffee and chatting with each other about the work that needs to happen that day. That organic kind of gathering speaks more to the strength of Clockwork's work culture than any holiday party ever could. {Minneapolis / St. Paul Business Journal Endnote 128}

Just three years ago, **HOK's** (#325) office space in St. Louis was a federal bankruptcy court with courtrooms that "looked like bad funeral-home chapels," recalls vice chairman Clark Davis. So when executives decided to renew their lease at Met 1, moving all of their employees to one floor, the world-renowned architecture firm did what it does best: transform the space into one of the most environmentally friendly offices in St. Louis. "We essentially created a loft-quality space inside a 20-year-old building," says Davis. Now the office is an airy environment with a prime view of the Arch and Busch Stadium that everyone can share. Stationed in rows of desks, architects and designers debate blueprints for a project in Saudi Arabia. "Almost everything we do is based on collaboration," says Davis, "so we wanted to encourage communication and bring people together." An open kitchen serves as a common meeting place. Glass-walled "huddle rooms" offer intimate spaces for employees to chat. Even 85-year-old founding partner Gyo Obata works inside a small cube surrounded by other creative minds. {St. Louis Magazine Endnote 129}

The young workforce at **Unruly** (#372), average age 29, thinks jobs are good for personal growth (90%). Aroon Sahani, a finance accounts assistant, joined as an intern. These would-be "unrulies" earn more than the minimum wage, get the first crack at any jobs coming up and meanwhile, get to eat the same croissants as the boss. Christian d'Ippolito, Group Head of International Sales, says:

> *"There's this energy in the company that makes everything exciting... there's a particular culture here, a tight sense of community and it's a lot of fun." Matt Cooke, CTO and a founder, says: "It's very collaborative and social. We aren't dictating — we are inclusive, and small things make a big difference, like a big kitchen." {Endnote 130}*

XPLANE (#708), which was founded in 1993, has an "Inspiration Wall" -- a designated space in the office kitchen where employees can post anything they have created or want to share that inspires them. "It helps us express new ideas and personal findings which foster surprising connections, creative collaborations and, at its simplest, helps us all know each other better." {Entreprenuer.com Endnote 131}

SLEEPING ON THE JOB

At **AOL** (#126) headquarters in NYC, perks include access to NapQuest, a specialized room where employees can grab some winks in "nap pods" and relax in one of many electronic massage chairs. {CBSnews.com Endnote 132}

GARDEN PARTY

Southern Ohio Medical Center (#111) started a garden and invited the staff to plant their own vegetables or come pick them on their lunch break. Consisting of two small greenhouses and several large raised beds, the garden turns out kale, broccoli, tomatoes, Brussels sprouts, rhubarb, strawberries, and lettuce. {World at Work Endnote 133}

LAGNIAPPE EXAMPLES: Beyond shelter, here are a couple of examples that address clothing:

Clothes make the Banker - Employees at **Umpqua Bank** (#42) are given $500 TWICE per year to purchase professional clothing for work. The amount is then deducted from their paychecks until paid in full in as little as $10 per paycheck. The result is no credit card interest. {cnn.money.com Endnote 134}

Dress Code - The right atmosphere is important. At **BBS Technologies** (#802), that means striving to replicate a college campus's freedom and intellectual excitement. The dress code at BBS? "You must wear clothes," explains CEO Rick

Pleczko. Otherwise, Pleczko said he wants everyone to feel comfortable at the software company as he tries to combine a casual atmosphere with a professional environment. "We care what you produce and deliver, but not so much how you look." {Houston Chronicle Endnote 135}

Transparency and Openness

"There are three requirements of a great workplace:
*1) Like the people you work with, 2) Do work that is
meaningful and 3) Trust the management.*"

- Dave Hitz of NetApp

Keying on #3 above, it begs the question, "How do you build trust?"

Let's look for guidance from India's **HCL Technologies** and Brazil's **Semco**.

Vineet Nayar, CEO of HCL Technologies, touched on trust in his bestselling book, *Employees First, Customers Second.* {Endnote 136} He outlines four ways that "Transparency builds Trust":

1. Transparency ensures that every stakeholder knows the company's vision and understands how their contribution assists the organization in achieving its goals. Working in an environment without transparency is like trying to solve a jigsaw puzzle without knowing what the finished picture is supposed to look like.
2. It ensures that every stakeholder has a deep personal commitment to the aims of the organization.
3. Gen Y members expect transparency as a given. They post their life stories in public domains; they expect nothing less in their workplaces.
4. In a knowledge economy, we want customers to be transparent with us, to share their ideas, their vision and their strategies for solving core problems. Why would customers be transparent with us if we don't trust employees enough to be transparent with them?

Transparency at Grupo Semco

Brazil's Semco is a great example of a democratic open environment with minimal hierarchy. The group of companies is headed up by CEO Ricardo Semler. According to British management guru Charles Handy,

> *"The way he works — letting his employees choose what they do, where and when they do it, and even how they get paid — is too upside-down for most managers."* {Endnote 137}

The company operates as an open book. In Semler's words,

> *Semco has no official structure. It has no organizational chart. There's no business plan or company strategy, no two-year or five-year plan, no goal or mission statement, no long-term budget. The company often does not have a fixed CEO. There are no vice presidents or chief officers for information technology or operations. There are no standards or practices. There's no human resources department. There are no career plans, no job descriptions or employee contracts. No one approves reports or expense accounts. Supervision or monitoring of workers is rare indeed... Most important, success is not measured only in profit and growth.* {Endnote 138}

Let's look at another Baker's Dozen of companies that go the extra mile to be open and transparent.

Open by Design

A visionary corporation, **W.L. Gore** (#46) is built from a blueprint that its founder refers to as a "lattice" (as opposed to a "ladder"). There is no visible hierarchy at Gore -- and no job titles. In fact, there are no bosses. Instead, there are leaders who achieve their positions by gaining followers. Business goals are established by consensus. Gore's internal "structure" was put into place in 1958 by cofounder Bill Gore, an ex-DuPont exec who believed, "leaders should be chosen by the people who follow them." {Fast Company Endnote 139}

If you join **Marina Maher Communication**s (#749), don't expect a title on your business card. "In our 28+years, we've never put titles on business cards," said Maree Prendergast, managing director-human resources and talent. "We always thought that limits people." In fact, its philosophy is "good ideas come from everywhere," said Marina Maher, founder of the PR agency. {AdAge.com Endnote 140}

Rule #1 of 5 Core Values: *Open Company, No Bullshit.* **Atlassian** (#47) embraces transparency wherever at all practical, and sometimes where impractical. All information, both internal and external, is public by default. "We are not afraid of being honest with ourselves, our staff and our customers." {Atlassian.com Endnote 141}

Feedback Plus (#59) has an open ledger policy for employees. They can read the company's financial statements any time they wish. Their compensation is based upon their work teams and the company's performance vs. the annual goals and action plans they've collectively developed. Of course it may not be feasible for every company to have an open ledger policy, but it is important that, whatever the size of the organization, each employee knows where they are going and how they're supposed to get there. {CareerCast.com Endnote 142}

Employees at **Catalyst Studios** (#288) say Founder Jason Rysavy's focus on finding like-minded colleagues and challenging work is what makes the firm a fun place to work. "My job and the job of the leadership here is to make sure the projects we're bringing in are satisfying for people to work on." The firm looks for challenging, unique projects in need of solutions, Rysavy said. "We tend to get these bastard-child projects that no one knows how to deal with, and we help figure it out." Over time, the firm has learned to turn down work that won't excite the agency's passionate problem-solvers. "The more you say no to the stuff that is clearly not a good fit for the people we have, the more the good stuff comes along."

Rysavy added, "We made a lot of money early on, but we did a lot of stuff that didn't get us anywhere. Delivering a product that clients and users can enjoy and that was satisfying to build is a reward beyond the 'smoke and mirrors' that other agencies use to keep their employees happy." {Minneapolis / St. Paul Business Journal Endnote 143}

Talent Plus + (#799) holds monthly business update meetings. Management shares financials with all employees in the spirit of transparency.

"Customer First News," an audio webcast that provides **Symantec** (#806) employees with updates on their NPS performance, actions being taken to address performance gaps and business results achieved. Symantec engages employees across the business in delivering this message, demonstrating that customer experience is owned by each and every employee. {Satmetrix.com Endnote 144}

AN OPEN DOOR

At **Flour Bakery + Cafe** (#136), none of the bakery manager offices have doors and all have anonymous suggestion boxes. "We try to create all sorts of ways to get feedback from the staff," says General Manager Aaron Constable. {boston.com Endnote 145}

Rand Corporation (#208) offers an open door policy at all levels of the organization. Anyone can make an appointment to meet with the CEO, Executive VP or any of the other VP staff. The company leadership host small group lunch meetings with open Q&A as well as coffee get-togethers for open Q&A. {Los Angeles Business Journal Endnote 146}

AnswerLab's (#510) CEO schedules Walk & Talks with every employee. These one-on-one check-ins provide employees with an individual opportunity to share any concerns or brilliant ideas they have with the CEO directly. Combining wellness with one-on-ones helps achieve two important objectives simultaneously. Meeting outside the office and getting physical helps eliminate the nerves and intimidation employees might normally experience when connecting with higher-ups. {GreatPlaceToWork.com Endnote 147}

Team One (#748) believes its "management by walking" practice and team camaraderie help maintain the culture at the agency. {AdAge.com Endnote 148}

Doug Conant, former CEO of **Campbell Soup Company**, (#248) took purposeful steps to be visible and promote good health at Campbell's. Doug took ten thousand steps per day to be exact in order to stay connected to employees. {HBR Endnote 149}

Everyone at the **Max Borges Agency** (#714) has the ability to discuss anything with anyone at the agency, where its "do not knock" policy is taken seriously. Taking that one step further, the company recently sponsored a four-week in-office communications course that was taught during regular business hours. It was based on a book titled "People Styles At Work," and its purpose was to enhance everyone's ability to effectively communicate with co-workers, clients and family. {PR News Online Endnote 150}

OVERTIME EXTRA

The **DRP Group** (#433) recognizes long hours working on videos, events, print and digital productions. "If the client pays for overtime, the team member will get 50% of what is charged." The policy has allowed some staff to make 30% extra per year. {The Sunday Times Endnote 151}

OPEN AND SECURE

National Instruments (#763) puts their employees first. "When other employers lay off in droves, NI hangs on, relying on cash they have consistently put away for the inevitable economic recession." – National Instruments Digital Hardware Engineer. {Glassdoor Endnote 152}

According to President David Martin of the **David Martin Agency** (#298), "We are different from other companies in our industry as we are salaried. By removing the commission-based compensation usually found in this industry, it allows all of us to enjoy the success of the individual performances. We celebrate our successes by announcing them company-wide. We share financial bonuses across all employees. Our philosophy is that sharing successes make our jobs even better!" {Minneapolis / St. Paul Business Journal Endnote 153}

STANDING UP FOR EMPLOYEES

Bad customers beware. **ING Direct** (#38) stands up to protect their employees. The bank has an operating strategy based on a strong, effective culture that is selective of prospective customers. It also requires the periodic "firing" of customers. At ING Direct, thousands are fired every month. This strategy is especially important when customers "abuse" employees or make unreasonable demands on them. {Endnote 154}

The rapidly growing **Belvedere Trading** (#165) gives both traders and its information technology staff opportunities to share ideas and take on new roles. "We want for every employee to feel an ownership in the firm, that they're going to have an impact on what we do," says Thomas Hutchinson, Belvedere Trading's president. "It's a flat structure," he adds. "No matter where they come from, ideas are taken with a serious attitude." Reflecting that flat structure, everyone in the firm, including interns, receives a bonus twice a year, which ranges from 5% to 200% of the employee's salary. {Chicago Real Estate Daily Endnote 155}

KEEPING IT ON THE LEVEL

Hilcorp's (#368) annual bonus is universal. There is a single set of targets and every employee is rewarded with the same percentage of his or her salary. The company shells out a maximum 60% bonus each year and has averaged 35% during the past five years. {The Houston Chronicle Endnote 157}

If **Integrated Project Management Company** (#547) exceeds its monthly profit targets, all employees receive the same bonus amount, regardless of position.

MAKING EMPLOYEES OWNERS

According to a quote on Publix.com, "**Publix** (#91) is an extraordinary company to work for. I've been here 36 years, my husband has been with Publix for 38 years, and my children have worked here as well. We love it because the people are warm and friendly, like our extended family; and because we own a part of the company. Mr. George, our founder, cared enough about associates to make all of us part owners."

Wenck Associates (#312) is a 100% employee owned company, backed by robust contributions to the plan, and has enjoyed healthy growth to the value of the company stock. The ESOP program and contributions provided are differentiators, helping Wenck to attract and retain members. From a financial performance standpoint, the company has an open book policy, sharing financial information monthly and at events throughout the year. Wenck provides a "self-directed training account" program, which allows employees to obtain additional development and training throughout the year to further their education and chase their dreams. There are many opportunities to grow, to be flexible and to have a balanced life.

The result: Employees are turning around and doing great things at Wenck. {Minneapolis / St. Paul Business Journal Endnote 158}

Shares went to all 82 staff at **Mount Anvil** (#408), allocated according to length of service, starting at £5,000. For Killian Hurley, the Chief Executive and Co-Founder, it was "the right thing to do." "There are lots of good companies, but we want to be excellent and to do that, you need engaged, positive people delivering excellent customer service. The share incentive is one of the little steps we can control; we are delighted to do it." {The Sunday Times Endnote 159}

The egalitarian ethos of this wholly employee-owned architecture practice **Make** (#424) is reflected in an annual profit share for all 111 staff. Everyone is a partner, and all feel fairly treated. It stands to reason that as owners, the staff insists on equitable pay. {The Sunday Times Endnote 160}

LAGNIAPPE: Semco has an interesting program. You don't need to wait until you're old to enjoy your retirement. The idea is that you can take advantage of it once a week, from any age. The *Retire a Little Bit* project (#190) was created based on a life-cycle analysis. In any analysis that we undertake, we see that we have money when we don't have time to enjoy it, time when we no longer have financial certainty and the ability to enjoy nature and sports when we no longer have the health to do so. The program allows the person to do what they plan to do when they retire, once a week, like taking an art course, playing sports in the afternoon or simply spending the day with their kids. The employee will have the option to not work one day a week, replacing this day in the future, after they retire, with a proportional salary. {Semco.com Endnote 161}

Chapter 14

WELLNESS, TIME AWAY & MODERN FAMILY

*"If there's a fountain of youth, it is probably physical activity.
Research has shown benefits to every organ system in the body.
So the problem isn't whether it's a good idea. The problem is how
to get people to do more of it."*

- Dr. Toni Yancey, Author of *Instant Recess*

WORKPLACE WELLNESS

The third inch on the 9 INCH journey to the heart of your employees involves wellness. Little extras designed to support healthy behavior in the workplace and improve health outcomes.

WHY IS WELLNESS SO BASIC?

Without health, we have nothing. It's an easy concept to grasp. More than just health, wellness is also about enhancing productivity. Max Borges of the **Max Borges Agency** (#713) breaks it down further,

> *"When you feel good physically,"* the triathlete says, *"you feel good mentally."*

Borge's South Florida company, does public relations for the consumer electronics industry, offers employee benefits such as an on site gym, as well as fitness classes and reimbursement for athletic competition entry fees. {DailyFinance.com Endnote 162}

Conversely, employees without a sense of wellness tend to take excessive sick days and suffer from low job satisfaction. Leaders at Canada's **Halton Healthcare** (#803) were faced with these exact issues. They found a solution in "*Kailo*," a decidedly psycho-social framework for staff wellness that was developed at Mercy Medical Center in Northern Iowa. Kailo, an ancient word meaning **whole**, pulls into balance all aspects of health and well-being, including social, emotional, spiritual and physical elements.

> *"We wanted to build trust and improve relationships among employees. Kailo offered proven approaches to demonstrate respect and value for all employees regardless of their current health practices, and allowed us also to promote humor, fun and play in the workplace," says Anna Rizzotto, Halton's Kailo Coordinator.*

Times of caring and sharing among co-workers were dubbed "Kailo" moments. Staff embraced all the benefits of Kailo, including "Kailo-to-Go" in-services, the Kailo Treat Kart, the Kailo First Aid Basket, and the ever-popular mini-massage. "The feel-good impact of mini-massage appears to surpass all other program offerings!" {Endnote 163}

TWO PATHS DIVERGE

As an employer you have two choices. Ignore wellness and pay a hefty premium (*pun intended*) or take action. Let's look at a baker's dozen of companies in the latter category. Organizations that demonstrate the ability to go the extra mile for workplace wellness.

FINANCIAL INCENTIVES

At **Kahler Slater** (#697), a Milwaukee-based architectural design firm, employees have access to health coaches and risk assessments. Individuals who meet health goals are rewarded with a discount of $720 off their annual health premiums. In addition, the firm sponsors a Wellness Committee that creates promotional and competitive activities to keep its 125 employees engaged. The committee works on three firm-wide activities per year, including charity weight loss challenges and events such as a "*Fast Food Challenge*," which encourages employees to avoid fast food for a month. {GreatPlaceToWork.com Endnote 164}

The wellness program at **Borshoff** (#719) includes subsidized yoga classes onsite, free pedometers, educational seminars and incentives to promote healthy living and positive work/life balance. Those who set and reach wellness goals receive $50 off their monthly insurance premium. The program has **91%** employee participation. {PR News Online Endnote 165}

Encouraging employees to consider alternative transportation, **Nature's Path Foods** (#641) offers $500 each year to spend on physical activities, such as the purchase of a new bicycle for commuting. The company also supports employees with secure bike storage and onsite shower facilities.

WINTER WELLNESS

There may be no such thing as a free lunch, but at **Anadarko Petroleum Corp.** (#355) there is a free flu shot. Recently, an in-house doctor started at the top of the company's 30-story office tower in The Woodlands and over three weeks worked his way down, floor by floor, giving injections to nearly **1,900** employees at their desks - at no charge. {Endnote 166}

Everyone at **First Response Finance** (#403) gets a "winter bag" packed with lip balm, an ice scraper, porridge, throat soothers, honey and lemon to see them through the darkest months. {The Sunday Times Endnote 167}

GYM DANDY

Some organizations have a company gym. Others may subsidize or pay for gym fees. **Reebok** (#4) took this to the next level in 2010 by converting a brick warehouse at Reebok's headquarters into an employee exclusive CrossFit "box" or workout center, with six coaches and extensive equipment [named CrossFit One]. About 425 employees at Reebok are taking part in Canton. This benefit reinforces the company's new mission: to get consumers moving. Participants lost over 4,000 pounds collectively during its first year. {Reebok Endnote 168}

In Canada, **Accenture** (#442) has an interesting perk for traveling employees. If offers the unique *"Athletic Minded Traveller"* program that includes reimbursement for use of hotel health clubs. {eluta.ca Endnote 169}

Great Little Box Company Ltd. (#496) has a corporate HQ that features a fully-equipped onsite fitness facility (with subsidized membership and personal training services), outdoor sand volleyball court, book exchange library, outdoor gazebo and rooftop deck, and even a dock for employees who wishing to commute by kayak to Mitchell Island. {eluta.ca Endnote 170}

Arc'Teryx Equipment Inc. (#623) provides employees with a wide range of onsite amenities including a fitness facility with an indoor bouldering cave. {Outside Magazine Endnote 171}

Gentle Giant Moving Company (#778), a small business based in Boston, has a unique wellness benefit. John Zimmer, an in-house chiropractor and renowned CrossFit trainer, works every day with movers, office staff and executives in a custom built CrossFit gym right inside of their warehouse. According to Mitch Curtis, "Our company has always focused on strength and fitness, but over the past few years, John has helped ingrain it even further in our company culture. Everyone here finds his services to be a HUGE benefit, as everyday gym access with a personal trainer can be quite expensive." {Gentle Giant Endnote 172}

THE FULL MONTY

Whole Foods (#77) pays 100% of healthcare premiums for its employees.

Alterian (#164) pays 99% of the premiums, covers deductibles of its medical plan and gives employees a $50 monthly health stipend that can be used for things like health club memberships and vitamins. {ChicagoBusiness.com Endnote 173}

Since 1988, **Starbucks** (#93) has offered full healthcare benefits to eligible full and part-time partners. All employees (yes - even part timers who work 20 hours a week) are eligible for health insurance benefits. In addition, the Thrive Wellness Campaign inspires Starbucks partners to take advantage of wellness opportunities and lead active, healthy lives, which, long-term, will help sustain comprehensive benefits at Starbucks. {Starbucks Endnote 174}

REIMBURSEMENTS AND STIPENDS

Employees at **Nerland** (#398) are reimbursed their entry fee once they successfully complete any sort of athletic achievement, such as a marathon, sprint-tri or bike race. {Outside Magazine Endnote 175}

Kashi (#404) offers employees health-insurance discounts for competing in sports leagues and a $400 stipend to spend on "natural healthy-lifestyle" products like a surfboard or cooking classes. {Outside Magazine Endnote 176}

LEVERAGING PROGRAMS AND ACTIVITIES

Groups of employees at **Root Learning** (#199) gather for yoga every Thursday evening in the company lobby.

Savings.com (#226) supports a healthy lifestyle. The office is currently participating in the P90x program, which is a 90-day commitment to health, body, mind and energy reserves. The company paid for the employees to get the P90x videos, which have become part of the company's library of books and DVDs. Savings.com provides a catered lunch for all employees every Tuesday. In addition, it has a fully stocked kitchen with snacks, drinks, and health conscious foods. {Los Angeles Business Journal Endnote 177}

Beyond building design and construction projects at **Clayco** (#320), many employees build toned bodies in a decked-out gym — complete with a personal trainer on the payroll. And after squeezing a quick workout into the day, they can shower off in bathrooms stocked with hairspray, Tums, mouthwash, floss and more. Trainer and wellness director Brian Imholz believes he's the only full-time trainer in the country with such a job. About one-third of Clayco's 350 local employees regularly work out at the gym.

> *"This is a place where you want to perform as well as you can, because you want to work for a company that takes care of you," says IT director Tom Dutton.*

When Dutton started at Clayco more than a year ago, he weighed 314 pounds. But he began regularly hitting the gym, drawing inspiration from quotes by Einstein and da Vinci painted on the company's walls. Now he glides on the elliptical machine while answering emails. So far, he's lost 104 pounds. {St. Louis Business Journal Endnote 178}

GOING THE EXTRA MILE FOR WELLNESS

As part of its employee support network, the fast-growing energy company **NuStar** (#10) makes the corporate jet available in times of crisis. In 2010, when an employee working on a construction project in the Caribbean needed medical attention for a pre-existing ailment, NuStar jetted him back to the States to see his personal physician. The company also dispatches the plane when needed to send employees to support a coworker in need -- flying employees from headquarters, say, to support a colleague in another location who had a death in the family.

Liberty Mutual (#180) offers *Best Doctors.* This free and confidential service is invaluable during those times when an employee or a family member receives a serious medical diagnosis. Through this program, founded by doctors affiliated with Harvard Medical School, you can consult with some of the world's top specialists to gain the insight and additional information needed to help confirm diagnosis and choose an appropriate treatment. {Liberty Mutual Endnote 179}

At **Dixon Schwabl** (#696), a Victor, NY based advertising and public relations firm, many of the company's 82 employees began considering whether or not to decline health benefits altogether rather than take on higher rates. In response, the firm introduced a sliding scale benefit for health and dental insurance. For employees with the lowest annual salaries, the firm covers the majority of health-care costs. Those making the highest salaries pick up more of the cost, with top earners paying up to 100% of premiums. {GreatPlaceToWork.com Endnote 180}

Balance is enforced at **BGT Partners** (#738). To further encourage a friendly workplace, employees are expected to say *"hi"* every morning and *"goodbye"* every night. BGT does it during reasonable hours, no less. According to CEO and co-founder David Clarke, all offices recognize a fairly strict 9-to-6 work schedule. "Our managers will walk around and kick people out if they're in the office any later. We want people to take care of themselves, and if you're not happy that's gonna start hurting your work." {AdAge.com Endnote 181}

Kaiser Permanente (#210) of Southern California sponsors bi-weekly farmer's markets at their campuses. The markets have included cooking demonstrations in the past by Kaiser Permanente. {Los Angeles Business Journal Endnote 182}

FUEL FOR THE WELLNESS FIRE

Collective Bias (#845) bought Nike Fuel Bands for the entire staff: Why? In the words of CMO Ted Rubin:

> *Nike's approach is brilliant and a new dimension in social marketing. People are engaging with its platform socially*

around its core brand promise. Nike has cleverly integrated its lines into Nike+ giving the user the ability to track specific shoes, but that's not the point. It has made its brand experience social and not in the 2009 way of adding Facebook likes, it actually integrated socialization into the product itself. Every run posted to Path or Tweeted reinforces the Nike brand promise whether the user was adorned with its products or not. After seeing the impact on Jay and myself, we decided to get Fuelbands for the entire Collective Bias team as holiday gifts. It will be interesting to monitor the impact of 50+ people challenging and goading each other to better health. I'd be willing to bet the ROI on such a purchase is enormous given the impact on overall fitness levels, awareness of daily activity and just the fun our folks will have interacting around the devices. We also look at this process as a way to not only socialize our team and have them experience social media marketing within our eco-system (an incredibly valuable learning experience), but as a relationship-building tool. These daily interactions bring the team closer; amplify the Collective Bias message that we care about employees and each other, and create company Brand Advocates, the best kind, who happily spread out new media ethos far and wide. {Ted Rubin Straight Talk Endnote 183}

Time Away

"Vacation days are like aspirin.
They only work if you take them."

- David Murphy, The North Face

A recent survey polled over 200 employees from 98 companies to find out what rewards they valued the most,

"Across all ages and cultures, time off was absolutely number one," according to Cindy Ventrice," author of *Make Their Day! Employee Recognition that Works.* {Endnote 184}

Time away from the office is not only valued by employees, its regenerative. Yet, Americans work an average of 47 hours weekly and average just two weeks of vacation a year. {Endnote 185} Those 10 days puts us dead last compared to all other developed countries.

Let's look at a Baker's Dozen of companies who place an emphasis on enabling employees to take time away from the office:

Managers at design firm **McMurry** (#512) receive quarterly reports that indicate how much PTO [Paid Time Off] their employees have taken along with their unused inventory. Employees are encouraged to take time off by their managers, while blogs and stories by the CEO reinforce the importance of time away. **Why it's great:** Making managers accountable for their team's time off helps ensure that workload is evenly distributed among teams, and that employees have the mental and physical energy they need to bring their best selves to work. **Why you should try it:** Unused vacation time costs employees and employers. Not taking vacation is shown to be detrimental to an employee's health and productivity, and yet many employees report losing unused vacation time or being afraid to request time off. {GreatPlacetoWork.com Endnote 186}

PAID, PAID VACATION

The CEO of Denver-based internet start-up **FullContact API,** (#19) said that in a market competitive for top talent, he wants to keep his employees happy and refreshed. The flip-flop wearing founder offers his employees $7,500 for what he calls "paid, paid vacation," however there are rules. "One, you actually have to take a vacation to get the money," Bart Lorang said. "Two, you have to disconnect from work, so that means no calls, no emails, no tweets, no work of any kind." Even Lorang admitted he has trouble following his rules. "I suck at it," he said. He has a picture with his fiancée, Sarah, at Egypt's great pyramids. Lorang is checking his email in the shot. Not surprisingly, employees said they loved having FullContact pick up the tab for their vacations. It's a real break for your brain. You come back refreshed and reinvigorated and more excited about the stuff you were working on when you left," said Robbie Jack, a FullContact API employee. {Yahoo.com Endnote 187}

Evernote (#81) recently changed their vacation policy to give people unlimited vacation. Employees can take as much time as they want, as long as they get their job done. In the words of CEO Phil Libin, "If you want to take time off, talk to your team, but we're still measuring you on the same thing, which is, did you accomplish something great? Frankly, we want to treat employees like adults, and we don't want being in the office to seem like a punishment. We always try to ask whether a particular policy exists because it's a default piece of corporate stupidity that everyone expects you to have, or does it actually help you accomplish something? And very often you realize that you don't really know why you're doing it this way, so we just stop doing it." Has the unlimited vacation policy working? "So far. We had to modify it slightly because one of the first things I started worrying about is whether people would actually take less vacation. I don't want people not to take any vacation because that's just bad for them, and it's bad for me. You're not going to get a lot of work out of someone if they haven't taken a vacation in a while. So we started rewarding people for taking at least a week at a time on a real trip by giving them $1,000 spending money. That seems to be going well." {New York Times Endnote 188}

MILESTONE REWARDS

A passport is required for this benefit. **New Belgium Brewery** (#392) rewards employees with a trip to Belgium with cofounder Kim Jordan on their fifth anniversary. {Endnote 189}

Employees at the consulting firm **Mark G. Anderson** (#273) enjoy an all expense paid trip to one of the Seven Wonders of the World for their ten-year anniversary. {Washingtonian Magazine Endnote 190}

This UK IT hosting provider **UKFast** (#421) provides a holiday allowance from 20 to 30 days. In the case of wedding bells in a given year, newlyweds get five extra days. {The Sunday Times Endnote 191}

Employees at **Element212** (#777) get three weeks vacation to start and their wedding anniversary off. {Todd Rimer Endnote 192} [*They are not responsible for reminding their employees of their anniversaries however*]

If unlimited vacation is not incentive enough, after five years of working for **Red Frog Events** (#796), employees are rewarded for their loyalty with a four-week, full-paid trip to Africa, Asia, Europe or South America for them and a friend. It's no wonder they only hire one in every 750 applicants who apply to work there. {TheGlobeandMail.com Endnote 193}

EXTERNSHIPS

Bain & Company (#715) offers several opportunities for employees to take a break from demanding roles to help them sustain long-term careers at Bain. These include externships, in which employees can enrich their business knowledge by taking up to six months to work for another company, and leaves of absence. {PR News Online Endnote 194}

Bank of Canada (#683) allows employees to work on exchange with other central banks and finance organizations. {eluta.ca Endnote 195}

Employees at the **Canadian Security Intelligence Service** (#684) can apply to take an unpaid leave of absence, extended unpaid education leaves of absence and even a self-funded leave of absence so employees can enjoy additional time-off with pay. {eluta.ca Endnote 196}

SABBATICALS

Kimpton (#6) is in the business of pampering guests, and it doesn't skimp on its staff, either. The San Francisco-based operator of 55 luxury boutique hotels provides one-month paid sabbaticals to managers and executive chefs who have been with the company for seven years. {CrainsNewYork.com Endnote 197}

Employees at New York, NY-based **Deloitte** (#197) don't have to sacrifice their life's dream for their careers because they enjoy the benefit of sabbatical leave. Deloitte offers four unpaid weeks off to do whatever they wish, and three to six months (yes, months) of partially paid leave to volunteer or pursue a career-enhancing opportunity. {Salary.com Endnote 198}

Every seven years, designer Stefan **Sagmeister** closes his New York studio (#461) for a year long sabbatical to rejuvenate and refresh their creative outlook. He believes the value of time off is often overlooked. {TedTalk Endnote 199}

Morningstar (#80) employees are eligible for generous sabbaticals. Six weeks paid time off every four years. In addition, employees can "take as much time as they want" for vacation. Rather than seeing that as a perk, employees were confused and tended not to take enough time. Now, the company specifies that the open vacation policy is defined as, "at least three weeks off." {TheDailyFinance.com Endnote 200}

Alcool NB Liquor (#676) offers a self-funded leave program that lets employees defer a portion of their salary and take extended time off for up to one year with pay. {ChicagoBusiness.com Endnote 201}

GENEROUS ALLOWANCES

Right out of the gate, **KPMG** (#125) offers five weeks off in year one of employment. {TheCareerRevolution.com Endnote 202}

Twenty-five vacation days per year from **Strava,** (#397) right from Day One. {Endnote 203}

Media Temple (#216) is a web hosting and software application services company. After only your third year of service, you are eligible to take a full month of paid vacation to renew and rejuvenate efforts. {Los Angeles Business Journal Endnote 204}

The biomedical software provider **5AM Solutions** (#254) offers eight weeks of vacation after ten years of service, the ability to telecommute at least once a week and three paid days a year to volunteer. {Washingtonian Magazine Endnote 205}

Modern Family

PUTTING FAMILY FIRST

Families have changed. Today's employers need to deal with issues such as same sex marriage, infertility, adoption, parental leave, day care, returning workers and eldercare. Making certain that employees can focus on their families reduces stress and keeps workers on a more even keel. This allows them to feel supported and focused on the tasks at hand.

According to a recent article by the New York Times,

> *"These kinds of benefits are a departure from the upscale cafeteria meals, massages and other services intended to keep employees happy and productive while at work. And the goal is not just to reduce stress for employees, but for their families, too. If the companies succeed, the thinking goes, they will minimize distractions and sources of tension that can inhibit focus and creativity."* {Endnote 206}

Let's look at a Baker's Dozen of companies that find ways to support today's modern family:

INCLUSIVENESS

Walgreen's (#51) embraces those with disabilities. Equality is at the core of Walgreen's hiring policy. More than just serving the shareholders, it's about serving each other and the community. {Endnote 207}

The London-based global tax and advisory firm **Ernst & Young** (#114), offers the same benefits for same-sex partners as for opposite-sex partners, even in states that don't recognize gay marriage. {salary.com Endnote 208}

ADOPTION AND INFERTILITY

Wendy's (#181) offers adoptive employees a combination of up to $24,300 in adoption assistance and up to six weeks paid adoption leave. {Dave Thomas Foundation Endnote 209}

CarMax (#85) offers assistance to help Associates build families through legal adoption. Qualified associates with one year of continuous full-time service are eligible to receive up to $4,000 in reimbursements for adoption-related expenses. {Endnote 210}

The law firm **Alston & Bird** (#9) builds a $25,000 fertility benefit into employees' health plans. The allowance includes coverage for treatments from in-vitro fertilization to less traditional options like acupuncture. {Endnote 211}

GETTING READY FOR BABY

Facebook (#20) gives employees $4,500 when they have a baby. A welcome little bonus for the new addition. {Endnote 212}

The tech giant **AOL** (#115) helps take the stress out of being a working parent by offering fringe family benefits to employees. To start, new moms receive prenatal instruction on everything from childbirth to newborn care through the company's *Well Baby Program*. New moms get eight fully paid weeks off for maternity leave. {Endnote 213}

The **University of Alberta** (#674) operates subsidized daycare facilities onsite for employees with young children and provides an offsite daycare subsidy up to $2,000 per child for employees looking for care closer to home. (Source: eluta.ca) {Endnote 214}

At **Eli Lilly** (#702) expectant mothers are allowed to take one month of paid leave *before* their due date. {Brazen Careerist Endnote 215}

McMurry (#694), a Phoenix-based marketing communications company, gives new mothers an $800 allowance for house cleaning, home health visits, meals, lactation consulting or other services. {GreatPlaceToWork Endnote 216}

DAY CARE

T-Mobile (#96) offers employees a childcare subsidy. According to their website,

> *"When your life is balanced, you bring more to the job and you are better able to help our customers. That is one of the key reasons we implemented a Childcare Subsidy Program. The program is designed to help you better balance work and life. Eligible employees can receive a monthly contribution to help with childcare bills."* {Glassdoor Endnote 217}

Bain & Company (#716) offers a backup child and adult care program called *Parents in a Pinch*, which provides access to in-home backup child care, either temporary or ongoing, any time an employee has a gap in regularly scheduled childcare arrangements.

The **McMurry** agency (#559) welcomes children at the office when day care isn't available. {BusinessInsider.com Endnote 218}

PARENTAL LEAVE

Aetna Life & Casualty Co. (#68) reduced resignations of new mothers by 50% by extending its unpaid parental leave policy to six months, saving the company one million dollars a year in training, recruiting and hiring expenses. "The reason so many of America's top companies offer paid parental leave is that it keeps workers loyal, and that holds down turnover costs," according to IWPR President Heidi Hartmann. "It's not generosity, its just good business." {Endnote 219}

The currency website **XE.com** (#444) offers parental leave for new fathers and covers up to 95% of salary for 35 weeks. {Endnote 220}

RETURNSHIPS AND MOM'S HOURS

AboutOne (#464) has a program for Stay at Home Mom's returning to the workforce. According to their website:

> *"Because we want to make it easier for these women to return to the corporate world, we have created AboutOne's Comeback Mom Returnship program. Similar to college internships, our Comeback Mom Returnships are for experienced professionals who want to rejoin the workforce. We offer flexible work arrangements on a trial basis to provide these 'on-rampers' with the opportunity to refine their skills and demonstrate their capabilities. Upon completion of the returnship, participants are evaluated for permanent employment with AboutOne."* {AboutOne.com Endnote 221}

Stew Leonard's (#94) offers "Mom's hours," enabling mothers to work while their children are in school - and take off the whole summer to be with them. School delays, no problem. {money.cnn.com Endnote 222}

All employees at **dePoel** (#516) are eligible to work part-time or in school hours only. {The Sunday Times Endnote 223}

SPOUSES AND KIDS

On an employee's birthday at **Studer Group** (#563), they receive a $75 gift card and $25 on their childrens' birthdays. {BusinessInsider.com Endnote 224}

Cresa Partners (#282) is an international corporate real estate advisory firm that exclusively represents tenants. They not only recognize each employee's birthday with a gift, they send spouses a gift on their birthday, as well. {Minneapolis / St. Paul Business Journal Endnote 225}

The oil and gas company **Anadarko** (#360) has a world-class fitness center. The center is free to employees and spouses, open early / late, open on weekends and offers personalized workouts and a host of exercise classes from yoga to Zumba. {Houston Chronicle Endnote 226}

RBA (#306) offers employees an annual allowance of "lodge credits," that can be used for the lodging portion of their family vacation. {Minneapolis / St. Paul Business Journal Endnote 227}

ELDERCARE

Flexibility and team support helps employees at Houston's **Hospice Compassus** (#380). The company recently received a special award because employee surveys consistently expressed this idea: "I feel genuinely appreciated by this company." Caring for employees dealing with the emotions of people facing the end of life for their family or themselves on a daily basis. Nurses, for example, can set their own schedules with clients. Lori Thomson, a registered nurse and executive director at the West Loop South office, says employees have access to the same bereavement workers and chaplains who work with clients. "Everybody feels for everyone else when a person is having a difficult time," Thompson said. "Hire great men and women who are talented, and treat them like family." {The Houston Chronicle Endnote 228}

According to **Goff Public** (#291) CEO Chris Georgacas, "We pride ourselves on being flexible to our team members' family schedules. That includes a three-month, fully paid maternity leave and "compassionate time" rather than a set number of sick hours. Compassionate time enables people to spend the time they need to with ailing family members, take good care of themselves and take care of other unexpected situations." {Minneapolis / St. Paul Business Journal Endnote 229}

The Canadian Uranium producer **Cameco** (#654) provides employees with compassionate leave top-up payments (to 100% of salary for 8 weeks) to workers who are called upon to care for a loved one. {eluta.com Endnote 230}

CustomInk (#695), a T-shirt and apparel company based in Tysons Corner, Virginia offers employees a dependent-care flexible spending account, which allows them to set aside $5,000 pre-tax for eldercare expenditures. {GreatPlaceToWork Endnote 231}

Chapter 15

TEAM BUILDING AND COLLABORATION

*"The greatest predictor of a team's achievement is
how the team members felt about each other.
The more team members are encouraged to socialize,
the more they feel connected."*

- Shawn Achor, CEO and Founder Good Think

The next three chapters cover the types of green goldfish associated with "BELONGING":

The fourth inch on the 9 INCH journey to the heart of your employees involves **Team Building**.

Success is frequently seen as a purely individual achievement, often at the expense of others. But in the corporate world, an organization can only thrive with the collective help of everyone. For employees, being part of a team helps create a sense of belonging. Feeling more connected leads to a greater level of happiness.

FOSTERING COMMUNITY

Assurance Agency Ltd., (#842) a Schaumburg-based insurance brokerage has a whole host of incentives. There's Starbucks coffee, yoga classes and a Wii station, plus big-ticket items such as referral bonuses for new clients, education reimbursements and companywide bonuses for reaching goals. Yet the benefits with the biggest impact on culture seem to be those that bring employees together. I think we're really thoughtful about the things we emphasize," says Jackie Gould, the company's chief operating officer. "A lot of them aren't really about the money. It's more about *fostering* the relationships." {ChicagoBusiness.com Endnote 232}

Let's look a Baker's Dozen of companies who actively foster a sense of community through Team Building:

Employees that play (music) together, stay together. **Harmonix Music Systems** (#133), maker of the game series Rock Band, goes the extra mile to support the company's bands by providing practice space. Down in the basement of their Cambridge headquarters, there's a hidden sanctuary where employee bands can rock out. The dedicated practice space is equipped with stage lights, music equipment and Christmas lights for mood. {boston.com Endnote 233}

Employees sit together in small, focused teams so collaborating is an ongoing process, although **Ubermind** (#741) encourages even more with competitions, lunch get-togethers and "*UberTalks*" -- a kind of client social for the firm and guests. In the words of Brooke Walker, VP of Finance and Administration, "A lot of really good engineers want challenges. They want to work on new and exciting projects, not legacy projects." {AdAge.com Endnote 234}

MAKE IT MEMORABLE

Decision Lens (#711) sponsors company excursions twice annually during working hours. They are completely paid for by the company. The founder worked at several large corporations and was turned off by what he called "lame" annual company barbeques or bowling excursions. He wanted to engage his employees with group activities and trips they otherwise may not be able to do on their own. For example, Decision Lens paid for its 35-person staff to visit the National Aeronautics and Space Administration's Goddard Space Flight Center about 20 miles northeast in Greenbelt, Md., where they listened to astronomers discuss how they've been using the Hubble Telescope. Last month, employees geared up for a day of competitive go-kart racing. According to CTO and co-founder Daniel Saaty,

"If you want to play paintball or go bowling, you can do that with your friends on your own time. The idea is to inspire people to do what they didn't think they could do. If an employee has a bad day or run of days, I want them to remember that these are the people that had his or her back and who shared an awesome, one-of-a-kind experience. That goes way beyond work." {Entreprenuer.com Endnote 235}

According to Rob White, CEO and Co-founder, **Zeus Jones** (#300), "Most Fridays, we have what we call '*Beer and Tell*,' where one or more people share what they have been doing with everyone on staff. The beauty of being a small company is that we can still all fit in a room, and celebrate the work, and the little or big successes of colleagues. In addition to our work for clients, these successes include new staff welcomes, engagements, pregnancies, babies, new pets and even winning debates with AT&T over cellphone bills. Big successes are celebrated with champagne — we write the occasion on the cork and keep all these marked corks in a jar." {Minneapolis / St. Paul Business Journal Endnote 236}

Healthy competition

At Virginia company **Snagajob** (#62), the Culture Squad organizes the annual Office Olympics, during which employees [Snaggers] are divided into competing nations—and dress the part.

Every four years, **Allianz** (#841) holds an international Olympics for its sports teams. The company covers the athletes' expenses and has an opening ceremony; in 2010, the games were held in Budapest with over 70 countries participating. {money.cnn.com Endnote 237}

For its hockey addicts, **PricewaterhouseCoopers Canada** (#458) hosts a unique national *PwC Hockey Tournament* with office teams gathering every spring for friendly competition and the chance secure bragging rights for the year. {eluta.ca Endnote 238}

IMPORTANCE OF PLAY AND PRANKS

It's not all work and high purpose at **OBS** (#349). The company is big on fun. Each office has a *Chief Fun Officer* whose responsibility it is to ensure that fun is also an important part of the business. According to one employee, "We don't take ourselves too seriously." {BRW Endnote 239}

Hit them with your best shot. When things get hectic and she gets that "I just want to scream feeling" about something or someone, Jennifer Callies of **Shazaaam! Public Relations** (#28) simply opens fire. Granted it's with a Nerf gun, but the release is very gratifying.

> *"We have a pretty small office and everyone gets along well and has a fun-loving spirit, so it was no surprise when our creative director went out one day and brought back Nerf guns for everyone," Callies says. "We take our frustrations out via Nerf wars."*

They shoot at walls, computers, phones, the damn copy machine and "from time to time, when the urge becomes contagious, we have it all out," she says. "It's an 'everyone for themselves' kind of war, using cubicles as hideouts and chairs as shields until all of our foam darts run out. After five to 10 minutes of heated battle with Nerf guns and childish fun, we are refreshed and ready to get back to work." {Keith Hein Endnote 240}

Coyne PR (#754) employees work hard, but they also know how to play hard together. The agency has a practice of harmless but hilarious pranks. Previous antics include placing 200+ balloons into the cube of a vacationing employee and switching the car keys of an unsuspecting co-worker. {CoynePR.com Endnote 241}

At **McNeill Designs for Brighter Minds** (#29), they take the time to just crack open a board game and play. "Maybe it's because we're a game development firm, but we find on a Friday afternoon, nothing beats playing a game," says CEO Donald W. McNeill. "We check out the competition and have a little healthy competition. We typically get a pizza and throw in a prize for the grand winner of the afternoon." Prizes vary from a "late morning start pass" to "party money." {Keith Hein Endnote 242}

OFFSITE ACTIVITIES

Each month **GoDaddy** (#110) places money toward off-site employee activities -- held during work hours -- to boost team morale. Recent activities for employees include whitewater rafting, gold panning, competitive cooking courses and trapeze classes. {WorldatWork.com Endnote 243}

Burton (#178) holds a *Fall Bash*, an annual party for Jake Burton's team, friends and family at his home, complete with a band, food, drinks and more. An annual day where the entire company rides together, BBQ's and has a few beers. {Mashable Endnote 244}

MENTOR PROGRAM

At **Allen & Gerritsen** (#736), even CEO Andrew Graff has a mentor. He's the youngest person at the agency, a 22-year-old emerging-technology strategist named Eric Leist. Of course, Mr. Graff is a mentor to the strategist, too. Every new employee is assigned one at the Boston-area agency, but senior folks aren't supposed to do all the talking. The arrangement makes even the most junior employees "reverse mentors," so everyone knows they can learn a thing or two. According to Graff,

> *"Don't just assume because you're more senior you're the mentor -- you could be the mentee. We strive for balance. It's a young-person business; tech is taking the business in new directions, so we need to listen to the young and fearless."*

So Mr. Graff gets schooled on why to check in to restaurants on Foursquare (for the tips) and how millennials use their phones (all the time). In turn, Mr. Leist gets sage marketing lessons from an executive with decades of experience. {AdAge.com Endnote 245}

Chapter 16

ATTABOYS AND ATTAGIRLS

"Teamwork is best accomplished when each team member feels valued and knows that they have a voice."

- Tom Coyne, Coyne PR

The fourth inch on the 9 INCH journey to the heart of your employees involves **Recognition**.

> *"YOU MATTER. These two words can change your mood, change your mind, and have the power to change lives and the world if we understand and leverage them in the right way."* {Angela Maiers, TED Talk June 2011 Endnote 246}

When I was in law school, I distinctly remember having a conversation with a classmate named John from South Carolina. John was telling me about his summer job working in a law office. I asked him if he'd considered staying on full-time after school. He shook his head, "No way." When I prodded John further he revealed that he had an issue with the partner that was managing him. "He doesn't give any attaboys." I had never heard the word "ATTABOY" before, but no explanation was needed. John felt that his work wasn't appreciated, nor recognized at the firm.

Recognition fuels a sense of worth and belonging in individuals. No rocket science here. As humans we crave acceptance. Dale Carnegie spoke of the importance of recognition nearly 80 years ago. Here are a couple of quotes from his classic, *How to Win Friends and Influence People,*

> *"Be lavish in your praise and hearty in your approbation. A drop of honey gathers more bees than a gallon of gall [vinegar]."* {Endnote 247}

RECOGNITION RESONATES

Thirty-five percent of workers and 30% of chief financial officers cited frequent recognition of accomplishments as the most effective nonmonetary reward. Thanking people for their hard work and commitment is key to making them feel appreciated. {Accountemps Poll Endnote 248}

SHIFTING A MINDSET

Most managers take an, "if, then" approach to recognition. Shawn Achor believes this paradigm needs to change, "...from thinking that encouragement and recognition should be used as rewards for high performance as opposed to thinking that encouragement and recognition are drivers of high performance." {The Happiness Advantage Endnote 249}

Let's have a look a Baker's Dozen of companies who give a little extra when it comes to employee recognition:

KUDOS AND SHOUT-OUTS

Every week **The Nerdery** (#305) agency compiles a video of shout-outs, with employees publicly praising their fellow nerds for going above and beyond. Five shout-out recipients are chosen for free lunches the following week. The weekly shout-out video is played for all at the Friday afternoon *Bottlecap Talk*, where the agency celebrates the successful launch of a recent project with a show-and-tell demo led by the rockstar developers who made it happen. {Minneapolis / St. Paul Business Journal Endnote 250}

Fishbowl Friday's are held each week at **LaBreche** (#301). Employees give kudos to each other for simple, everyday things that are done extraordinarily or out-of-the-park big hits. {Minneapolis / St. Paul Business Journal Endnote 251}

BESPOKE AWARDS

According to Wellsphere, **Valtech Software** (#916) circulates a stuffed elephant for co-workers who are positive in attitude or action. The program was initiated by developer Michael Poulsen. {Endnote 252} Poulsen volunteered to be Chief Happiness Office. Here is how he presented the program to the team:

Purpose:
To bring all the good things we do for each other out in the light.

How it works:
The elephant is passed on from co-worker to co-worker on a weekly basis, with a reason why it is passed to that person in particular.

The reason for passing the elephant on to a new co-worker is up to you. Maybe someone helped you move apartment, fix a bug in your code or just have a positive impact on your day by always being happy and smiling.

Ground rules for elephant care:

1. An elephant is given to a co-worker for a good reason (i.e., having a good attitude or doing something helpful).

2. The recipient must be told why he/she has been awarded the elephant.

3. The elephant can only be kept for one week, and it must be displayed for all to see.

4. Someone is in charge of the overall elephant tracking.

Rackspace (#435) created a special award for employees who are fanatical about serving customers. It's simply called *The Jacket*. It signifies fanaticism and hence is a straightjacket. Only one employee wins the jacket at a time. {YouTube Endnote 253}

The Container Store (#459) has an award called *The Gumby*. Being Gumby is about doing whatever needs to be done to serve a customer, help a co-worker or complete a task. It's about not getting "bent out of shape" when a customer makes a request of you that you'd rather not do. And it's also about bouncing back quickly after having a tough encounter with a challenging customer. Every Container Store employee is strategically trained to think flexibly to solve customers' organization problems. And the company does this with an air of excitement by using the 1950's Gumby clay-figure TV star. The company constantly reinforces the Gumby culture by having a 6 foot tall wooden Gumby in the lobby at the company's headquarters and giving away the annual Gumby award to the employee who exemplifies flexibility. {Myra Golden Endnote 254}

Decision Lens (#712) awards top-performing salespeople with *custom-made action figures* designed to resemble the employee. According to Co-Founder John Saaty,

> *"It's a humorous way to acknowledge the great efforts of our sales team, and something that's more memorable than the usual plaque or something like that."* {Entrepreneur Endnote 255}

Executives at **Zappos** (#122) pick a *"hero"* each month and award them with a parade, covered parking spot for a month, a $150 Zappos gift card and a cape. {YouTube Endnote 256}

Marco (#308) distributes quarterly and annual *C.A.R.E. (Customers Are Really Everything) Awards* to employees who are selected by their peers for outstanding performance in teamwork, customer satisfaction and innovative ideas. Winners receive gift packages and award certificates and recognition at Marco's annual shareholders meeting. Being employee owned also helps Marco attract and retain long-term employees who understand the relationship between the company's success and our customers. The "think like an owner" attitude of employees is demonstrated through the long-term relationships they've developed with clients over the years. {Minneapolis / St. Paul Business Journal Endnote 257}

At this social game and advertising company **RockYou** (#144), good ideas are recognized every six weeks with the *YouRock Awards*, hosted at the company's all-hands meetings. The YouRock Awards started as a way to promote a bottom-up employee nomination process so people could recognize those whom they work with daily. Driven by peer nominations, RockYou awards teammates for solving a problem, designing a game, demonstrating innovation and exhibiting behaviors aligned with the RockYou values. YouRock nominees spin a wheel to choose an award such as cash, concert tickets, an extra day off or an iPad. All YouRock recipients also receive a *Golden Bobble-head Cow* trophy, offering them desktop bragging rights. The open forum in which people can be recognized and recognize others fosters a compassionate and playful company culture. {Mashable Endnote 258}

Our coveted peer-nominated *Water Carrier* award at **CamelBak** (#430) is presented annually to a group of employees who uniquely embody and transfer company culture and values to other associates. The award is named in honor of the Native American tradition of carrying water to fellow tribe members to sustain life and provide one of the essential elements for survival. {Outside Magazine Endnote 259}

The **Tabar** (#411) *Thumbs Up Award* is a roaming statue that sits on an employee's desk when he or she goes over and above the call of job performance. {Outside Magazine Endnote 260}

Martin | Williams (#307) gives out an annual award called *The Ribble*, which is a trapeze term for a great catch, something the audience just expects. It goes to people who day-in and day-out come to work and do such a good job that people come to really depend on them in ways that almost blind them to their importance. They represent the best of our culture. {Minneapolis / St. Paul Business Journal Endnote 261}

You may not need to wear formalwear to pick it up, but if you're caught doing great work at **Undertone** (#745), you may win an "Undertonie." It's just one-way the digital advertising company Undertone encourages and rewards creativity. There are also weekly massages, manicures and a free-beer cart. {AdAge.com Endnote 262}

IMMEDIATE RECOGNITION

Each **SC Johnson** (#530) office has its own Now Thanks! Program. The program provides on-the-spot recognition for great work with praise and a monetary award. {businessinsider.com Endnote 263}

American Express (#532) has a *Prize Patrol*. A group of four or five leaders get together and surprise their coworkers with flowers or a gift in front of their colleagues to celebrate their accomplishments. {businessinsider.com Endnote 264}

TAKE NOTE: THE BEST THINGS IN LIFE ARE FREE

A recent study confirmed that the cost of recognition awards has only minimal impact on employee perception of appreciation. Fifty-seven percent reported that the most meaningful recognition was free. Just look at some of these quotes to judge the impact:

> *"I received a hand written thank you in the mail from my manager and my CEO. I smiled like an idiot." - Bill A.*

> *"I got a bonus with a handwritten note. I read the note several times; even took a picture of it. Bonus was good too, but no picture." - David H.*

"Because few people expect much in the way of reward these days, a small but personalized thank-you can have a big impact," says Steve Richardson, founder of Diverse Outcomes and former chief talent officer for American Express. "Even when I send a recognition note to a big group or team, I try to add a personalized paragraph in each person's email, so it's highly tailored to the individual." {HBR Endnote 265}

Former CEO of the **Campbell Soup Company** (#21) Doug Conant is a big proponent of the power of handwritten notes. In Doug's words,

> "Look for opportunities to celebrate. My executive assistants and I would spend a good 30 to 60 minutes a day scanning my mail and our internal website looking for news of people who have made a difference at Campbell's. Get out your pen. Believe it or not, I have sent roughly 30,000 handwritten notes to employees over the last decade, from maintenance people to senior executives. I let them know that I am personally paying attention and celebrating their accomplishments. (I send handwritten notes too because well over half of our associates don't use a computer). I also jump on any opportunities to write to people who partner with our company any time I meet with them. It's the least you can do for people who do things to help your company and industry. On the face of it, writing handwritten notes may seem like a waste of time. But in my experience, they build goodwill and lead to higher productivity." {HBR Endnote 266}

The managing partner at **Windes & McClaughry** Accountancy (#220) actually handwrites all employee welcome, birthday and anniversary cards. He also gives a red rose to female employees and cookies to male employees on Valentine's Day. {Los Angeles Business Journal Endnote 267}

Plan B Technologies (#266) attributes its success to going the extra mile for clients, and it does the same for staff. Employees enjoy fully paid health-care premiums, an $85 monthly contribution to a health savings account, regular telecommuting, quarterly awards, spot bonuses, frequent free meals and handwritten thank-you notes from the CEO. {Washingtonian Magazine Endnote 268}

Long before he became CEO of **iProspect** (#739), back as an analyst at Bain Capital and KPMG, Robert J. Murray had an idea on how you should run a services business. "One thing that always surprised me in prior work experiences is when your assets walk out the door each day, why aren't companies doing more to value the people doing the business?" Mr. Murray thinks he's found the answer to that, and quite a large number of his employees happen to agree. Mr. Murray's formula: hire competitive people; promote early and often; give constant feedback, including *iProps* -- notes of encouragement. "We are a meritocracy. When positions come open, we don't care if you've been here six months or six years -- we will promote the best person into that position," he said. {AdAge.com Endnote 269}

Thank you Thursdays at **Professional Placement Resources** (#511) fosters a culture of gratitude that extends to clients as well. On Thank you Thursdays, the CEO asks employees to send a specific number of thank you notes to both internal and external customers. {Great Place to Work Endnote 270}

Recognizing Milestones

The tenure program at **Sweetgreen** (#140) called *Shades of Green* has blown up into a competition and become a status symbol among employees. Every teammate gets a free shirt, and the longer you're with Sweetgreen, the darker your shirt. Who knew a free t-shirt could help to shape company culture? After a teammate has been with Sweetgreen for one year, you also get a pair of green high-top Converse sneakers. At two years, you get a t-shirt and a neon green iPod Nano Touch. After three years, you get a lime-green Sweetgreen bike. {Source: Mashable Endnote 271}

Clif Bar (#152) was born on a bike. Every employee in the company received a bike on the 20th anniversary of the company.

My close friend told me about her friend's first week working at **O Magazine** (#16). In addition to being an awesome gig, she got a

$10,000 check and an iPad on her second day there. I first assumed that it was a good sign on bonus; however, she explained that it was not. Rather, it was just incredible timing; it was a onetime thank you gift Oprah gave to all the staff despite how long they have been with the company. {Bryan Welfel Endnote 272}

Every significant anniversary at the **St. Regis Hotel** (#373) is acknowledged with a party, a plaque and a gift from Tiffany. {Houston Chronicle Endnote 273}

Employees at **Harbinger Partners** (#285) receive a gift each month. Grausnick has distributed gifts that range from a Harbinger umbrella to flowers to iPads to big-screen TVs. "It's just really, really nice," said Cindy Smith, Harbinger's finance administrator. "It's so much fun to get some mail. It's all about the little things they think of." {Minneapolis / St. Paul Business Journal Endnote 274}

The **Hotze Health & Wellness Center** (#344) gives employees a piece of Waterford crystal to mark key accomplishments and anniversaries. Every new employee, including accountants and publicists, must pass an exam on the first try that shows they understand the entire treatment regimen at the clinic. It's stressful, especially for those who aren't used to the medical terminology, so Hotze likes to recognize the accomplishment with a piece of crystal from Waterford, said Christy Hammett, assistant director of public relations and marketing. Each staff member gets two more pieces - typically wine goblets or Champagne flutes - at the annual Christmas party and on their yearly anniversary they receive another, Hammett said. Patterns are assigned based on availability. Founder and CEO Steven Hotze, a longtime fan of Waterford crystal, wanted to give his employees something they'd treasure and pass down through the generations, said Hammett, who has amassed six or seven Champagne flutes in the Elberon pattern. She brings them out when she entertains, as she did earlier this year to toast her engagement. "I didn't even register for crystal," she said. "I'm getting that at work." The perk began 21 years ago and impresses job applicants as well. "They get so excited when they get the first one." {Houston Chronicle Endnote 275}

Brady, Chapman, Holland's (#369) *Diamond* program encourages generosity in daily work life. When a BCH employee does something exceptionally well for a client, fellow employee or the community, an acrylic diamond is tossed in a jar. Once the jar fills up, they celebrate by playing a game or going to a sports bar. {Houston Chronicle Endnote 276}

LAGNIAPPE: Roger Staubach once said, "There are no traffic jams along the extra mile." How about this example of going "above and beyond" to help an employee? One of the agency principals at **Mantis Pulse Analytics** (#366) was alerted that an employee was having major car issues. He then went on Craigslist and bought a transmission. He towed the employees Jeep to his house and fixed it.

Chapter 17

FLEXIBILITY AND CONTROL

"It's not just the number of hours we sit at a desk
that determines the value we generate.
It's the energy we bring to the hours we work."

- Tony Schwartz, CEO of The Energy Project

The sixth inch on the 9 INCH journey to the heart of your employees involves **Flexibility**.

Flexibility is about control and everyone wants flex. According to the Center for Talent Innovation's research, if there's one work perk that rises above the rest, it's flexible work arrangements. The CTI study showed that 87% of Boomers, 79% of Gen X'ers and 89% of Millennials cite flex as important. {CTI Endnote 277}

Why be flexible? The bottom line benefit for companies is increased productivity and job satisfaction. According to Sylvia Ann Hewlett,

> *"Companies that treat time as currency — through remote work options, staggered hours, and reduced-hour arrangements — are also more likely to attract and retain high-caliber employees. Work/life balance has always been prized by working women juggling the demands of family and high-powered jobs, and now these moms are being seconded by incoming Millennials, who consider it a basic entitlement to play as hard as they work."* {hbr.org Endnote 278}

A CHANGING WORKPLACE

By some estimates perhaps one-quarter of all US jobs could be performed remotely, and in a 2011 survey of 2,000 US businesses, one-quarter of them said they planned to use more remote workers in the future. {McKinsey Endnote 279} Forty percent of U.S. workers have jobs that could be done from home at least part of the time. {Telework Research Network Endnote 280} It's already happening. Regular telecommuters at Cisco and Accenture employees exceed 80% of their workforce. Many tech experts are convinced we won't even need offices as we know them in the future. {Fortune Endnote 281}

WORKSHIFTING BY THE NUMBERS

Citrix has pioneered the concept of **Work·shift·ing**. Work·shift·ing is using the web to get work done anytime, anywhere — outside the traditional office space. It produces savings for employees, employers and the environment:

- Workplace flexibility can save employers up to $20,000 per employee per year.

- Workshifters save between $4,000 and $21,000 per year in travel and work-related costs.

- 80% of employers say workshifting options help recruit talent.

- Companies with telework policies realize an 18% savings in real estate, electricity and office expenses.

- Half-time telecommuting nationwide would spare the environment the equivalent of taking 10 million cars permanently off the road.

Increasing business performance and employee satisfaction

- Workshifters are 55% more engaged than non-workshifters.

• When telework policies are introduced, companies report a 25% reduction in employee attrition.

• Workshifting increases productivity by 27%.

• 72% of employees say flexible work arrangements would cause them to choose one job over another.

• Turnover for employees who do not have the flexibility is almost twice the rate of those who do. {Citrix Endnote 282}

Let's look at a Baker's Dozen of companies who push the limits of Flexibility:

Patagonia Inc., (#35) based in California, attracts outdoorsy types with its athletic clothing brand and laser-like focus on work-life balance. Time away from the office isn't just tolerated here, it's required, says Rob BonDurant, Patagonia's Vice President of Marketing and de facto culture guide. Its 1,300 employees enjoy what the company calls "Let My People Go Surfing" time -- a period during any work day where employees can head outdoors to get their creative juices flowing. Of course, they can't abandon their duties or ditch a meeting, but popping out for an impromptu climb or bike ride is encouraged. Patagonia's flextime policies -- which originated from Yvon Chouinard, an outdoor enthusiast who founded the company in 1974 -- are good for employee morale and invaluable to the company.

In the words of BonDurant,

> *"The time we spend outside the office helps us manage the storytelling process around our products. We're designing ski and surfing apparel, we need to be traveling and trying things out."* {Entrepreneur.com Endnote 283}

Patagonia (#188) also gives employees two weeks of full-paid leave to work for the green nonprofit of their choice. {Endnote 284}

CONTROL OF HOURS / SCHEDULE

Managers struggle to judge employees on outcomes, not hours, since defining clear goals and determining reasonable time lines are difficult.

According to JetBlue's VP of Talent Bonny Simi,

> *"Bosses need to just relax. They don't have to see the employee for the work to get done. That's the hardest shift in mind-set for some managers. They [employees] don't want to work 9 to 5 ... and it doesn't matter to me if they work better from six at night until three in the morning or if they can do the work in six hours instead of eight."* {McKinsey Endnote 285}

Work schedule flexibility is a major reason employees prefer working at **Busch Gardens** (#364). It has helped make the Tampa Bay theme park a go-to employer. According to David Bode, VP of Human Resources, "We learned how to be very flexible because we employ a lot of students with strange hours and people who rely on us for second jobs. Plus our work demand varies so much."

Busch needs a minimum of 1,500 people to keep the place open seven days a week. They bulk the staff up to 4,500 for the peak summer and winter seasons between Christmas and Easter. But needs vary dramatically with weather, the day of the week, the time of day and attendance projections, so the park has made schedule juggling an art form. "It's great," said Chris Noyce, a 21-year-old USF environmental sciences major in his third year as a ride operator. "When you work is almost up to you."

Employees post their availability on a company website. Shifts are pared down to work units of four to six hours. The computer matches available employees to attendance projections and work demands two weeks ahead of time. The supervisors then fine-tune and juggle the actual work assignments — even down to the same day. {Tampa Bay Tribune Endnote 286}

At **Brand Learning** (#333) directors are trusted to manage their time and way of working, within reason, and there are reduced work options of 2½, three and four-day weeks. {The Sunday Times Endnote 287}

Believe it or not, **Point B** (#279), a Portland management consulting company, offers its employees no paid vacation time or holidays — and the employees seem to love it. That's because this company believes so firmly in flexibility that associates get paid only for the time they work, so there is no arbitrary limit to how much time off they can take. "I've never worked anywhere that was as committed to helping employees realize what the work-life balance means to them individually," says one employee. {Oregon Business Endnote 288}

The furniture retailer **IKEA** (#603) offers a range of alternative work options to help employees balance work-life commitments, including flexible hours, shortened and compressed work week options and job-sharing arrangements. {Endnote 289}

Lori Ames at ThePRFreelancer.com (#773) has a small business with two employees. In her words, "One of my employees is dating a New York City police officer, who works 5 days on, 2 days off, 5 days on, 3 days off. I've structured her schedule so that she works the same days as he does and is off for 2 days each time he's off. Sometimes her weekend is M & T, sometimes S & SU; but it's made for a very happy employee." {Lori Ames Endnote 290}

Up and Down Pay at **Semco** (#785). If an employee is going through a phase in which they would rather work less and accept lowering their pay accordingly, the company is committed to do its best to adapt. {Fortune Endnote 291}

REMOTE ACCESS

All employees at **Fulcrum Inquiry** (#222) receive a laptop computer, plus remote access to all of the firm's technology and files. All employees can work remotely if their particular assignment at that time makes this practical. All employees occasionally work remotely. A few employees extensively work from home and during non-standard hours. Workers also boast a Flexible Schedule. Consultants own their schedule based on client needs. {Los Angeles Business Journal Endnote 292}

Flexibility is the norm at this accounting firm. **PwC** (#233), with more than 160,000 employees operating in 154 countries, has one of the highest percentages of telecommuters — with 70% of employees working from home at least 20% of the time. {Atlanta Business Chronicle Endnote 293}

ROWE, ROWE, ROWE YOUR OFFICE

At most companies, going AWOL during daylight hours would be grounds for a pink slip. Not at **Best Buy** (#13). The nation's leading electronics retailer embarked on a radical --if risky--experiment in 2005 to transform a culture once known for killer hours and hard-riding bosses. The endeavor pioneered by Cali Ressler and Jody Thompson, called ROWE, for "***Results-Only-Work-Environment***," seeks to demolish decades-old business dogma that equates physical presence with productivity. The goal at Best Buy is to judge performance on output instead of hours. The program aims to weed out "presenteeism": the problem of employees warming their chairs all day but not getting much done. There are no schedules. Hence, workers pulling into the company's amenity-packed headquarters at 2 p.m. aren't considered late. Nor are those pulling out at 2 p.m. seen as leaving early. No mandatory meetings. No impression-management hustles. Work is no longer a place where you go, but something you do. According a study of workers by the University of Minnesota, it was a win-win proposition. Productivity and job satisfaction both increased by over 30%. {Business Week Endnote 294} [**R.I.P** – CEO Hubert Joly just abolished ROWE on 3.4.13] {Endnote 295}

Netflix believes that "Hard Work is Not Relevant." According to CEO Reed Hastings,

> *"We don't measure people by how many hours they work or how much they are in the office. We do care about accomplishing great work. Sustained B-level performance, despite "A" for effort, generates a generous severance package, with respect. Sustained A-level performance, despite minimal effort, is rewarded with more responsibility and great pay."* {Endnote 296}

Jeff Gunther, CEO of the Charlottesville **Meddius** (#182), VA-based software company Meddius, decided he would change the way his staff works by instituting a Results-Only Work Environment. Meddius employees can work any time from any place in any way, as long as they get their work done. Gunther has found that by giving employees the trust and autonomy they need, they've actually been more productive and loyal to the company. {Inc.com Endnote 297}

Edmunds.com (#203) boasts an innovative corporate culture, highlighted by a rollout of a Results-Only Work Environment in 2012. Under ROWE, Edmunds.com employees are offered the freedom to work at any time from any location where they can most effectively deliver their expected results. {Endnote 298}

In the words of Matthew DiGeronimo, Principal at **Smith Floyd** (#772)

> *"I enforce NO work hours. Performance driven - not hours logged driven. Employees can even attend staff meetings from home (via Skype) if they desire."* {Smith Floyd Endnote 299}

PERKS / CONCIERGE

At **S.C. Johnson** (#200), 12,000 employees have access to a concierge service that will take care of just about any chore: from returning overdue library books to making sure your dry cleaning gets picked up on time. The Wisconsin based company is in the business of cleaning products, after all. {The Fiscal Times Endnote 300}

During the firm's busy season, a *perk* plan is offered at **RBZ, LLP** (#212). Weekly manicures, massage therapy, daily catered dinners, nightly office-wide Trivial Pursuit games, espresso cart and free hotel stays nearby. A full-time concierge runs errands, and a free house cleaning each three-month season rounds out this incredible benefit. {Los Angeles Business Journal Endnote 301}

Benefits are first class at **Counterpart International Inc.** (#722). In addition to health insurance and a 403(b) fund, the organization offers three lifestyle benefits (employees are allowed to choose one): gym membership, a $125 public transportation benefit or paid parking in the building's garage. {PR News Online Endnote 302}

JOB ROTATION

Employees at **MERS/Missouri Goodwill Industries** (#329) can try on various positions for the best fit. {St. Louis Business Journal Endnote 303}

"Orionites," as they call themselves at **Orion Trading** (#742), don't like to stay in one place. The company encourages employees to try different jobs from time to time, moving in and out of marketing, sales, client services or media investment. The goal is to grow employees skills, which Orion has found increases everyone's output. {Advertising Age Endnote 304}

WORKING OFF-SCRIPT

From a post by Jay Baer at Convince & Convert:

Mid-way on a **Southwest Airlines** (#521) flight home from a speaking engagement in Ft. Lauderdale, I looked up from my laptop to find Becky the flight attendant standing at the front of plane with a boy of about 9.

'Ladies and gentlemen, I'm sorry to disturb you, but I just thought you should know that we have a celebrity on the plane today. Well, perhaps not a celebrity today, but someday this young man will be a famous artist. Abraham has drawn us a marvelous picture. It's quite wonderful, and I'll be displaying it up here so we all can enjoy his great picture.'

The kid was absolutely BEAMING with pride and accomplishment and happiness and honor. Abraham returned to his seat. Becky broke out the medical kit, ripped open a band-aid and used it as ersatz tape to post the picture on the wall.

A few minutes later, Abraham was back with a second picture. A landscape this time, Becky again made an announcement and grabbed another band-aid.

When I talk about focusing on BEING social, rather than focusing on DOING social media, this is what I mean.

Social business isn't about tools and technology. It's about giving Becky the freedom to work off-script. It's about cultural DNA that values moments of delight. It's about treating customers as humans, not transactions. It's about winning hearts and minds one planeload at a time with a personal, shared experience.

And it's about building loyalty and triggering word-of-mouth by doing it well. Will Abraham's parents ever fly any other airline? Will he? Will I? Or you?

For companies that are social at their core, social media just lets the rich get richer. For companies that don't truly believe in the primacy of the customer, all the Twitter and Facebook and blogs and YouTube in the world won't change their fortunes.

Social is foremost a philosophy, not a set of behaviors. And actions speak louder than words." {Endnote 305}

FLEXIBILITY WITH KIDS

Schools Financial Credit Union (#103) allows any of its employees to bring their newborns to work until the children are six months old. According to the Vice President of Marketing at the company, the babies cause little distraction, and since the parents can continue performing most of their work duties, the company doesn't have to hire temps or train new people. {Quality Logo Products Endnote 306} **SFCU** (#766) also supports a program called *School Activities Leave*. Employees may take up to 40 hours per year off for participation in a child's school activity.

Hot Studio (#877) worked closely with the Parenting in the Workplace Institute, a non-profit based in Salt Lake City, Utah, to create their *Babies-at-Work* program. The Institute helps organizations start successful programs and maintains a growing database of more than 140 workplaces around the country that allow babies at work. Baby-inclusive organizations report higher morale and retention, increased teamwork, an easier transition back to work for new parents, enhanced client loyalty, and greater interest from job applicants.

According to Principal, Program Planning and new Mom Courtney Kaplan,

> *"Dividing my life into separate roles at work and at home is stressful. It's nice to have a program at Hot that offers a more integrated choice. The office is the new village."*

Hot Studio has implemented a structured, formal *Babies-at-Work* policy with specific provisions to ensure that all employees' needs are taken into account and that the babies are not disruptive to the efficient functioning of the company. The agency views its babies-at-work program in line with its other programs that accommodate employees' volunteer interests and other family needs. Especially in these difficult economic times, Hot Studio is proud to offer a program to its employees that eases the substantial burden of high infant day care costs and the all-too-common—and grueling—situation in which parents must separate from their newborn babies, at a few weeks or months of age, to return to their jobs.

In the words of Hot Studio's CEO and Founder, Maria Giudice,

> *"I managed to grow a company and raise two children of my own in the 13 years of being in business. I brought my babies to work until they were each eight months old and I'm happy to see other new mothers doing the same. We are proud and thrilled to be affiliated with the Babies-at-Work Program."* {Hot Studio Endnote 307}

LAGNIAPPE: This is a brilliant creative move by Hot Studio. The company has purchased a soundproof booth that will serve the dual purposes of a quiet space for parents to take fussy babies as needed and, when parents and babies aren't using the booth, a place for video sound editing for client projects.

FLEXIBILITY WITH PAY AND BENEFITS

All employees at **Darden** (#86) Restaurants (Red Lobster, Olive Garden, LongHorn Steakhouse, The Capital Grille, Bahama Breeze, Seasons 52, Eddie V's) are eligible for health insurance and disability coverage from the first day of employment, which is highly unusual in the restaurant business. In addition, Darden pays employees on a weekly basis, rather than bi-weekly – even though it costs them more to do so – because they recognize the economic needs of their workers. {Endnote 308}

Unlike many technology and management consulting companies,

Jabian Consulting (#245) focuses on local client engagements, meaning its consultants do not endure the typically grueling travel demands that often come with consulting work. {Endnote 309}

FLEXIBLE DRESS CODE

Several winning workplaces stress the importance of the right atmosphere. At **BBS Technologies** (#802), that means striving to replicate a college campus's freedom and intellectual excitement. The dress code? "You must wear clothes," according to CEO Rick Pleczko. Otherwise, Pleczko said he wants everyone to feel comfortable at the software company as he tries to combine a casual atmosphere with a professional environment, "We care what you produce and deliver, but not so much how you look," {Houston Chronicle Endnote 310}

Chapter 18

TRAINING AND RETIREMENT

"Learning at Accenture is changing people's lives;
its giving them more reason than ever to stay
with us and grow both personally and professionally."

- **Jill Smart**, Accenture

The next three chapters will cover the types of green goldfish associated with "BUILDING":

The seventh inch on the 9 INCH journey to the heart of your employees involves **Training and Development**. Let's look at a Baker's Dozen of companies that go the extra mile to build employees through T+D:

Evernote (#83) has a program called *Officer Training*. CEO Phil Libin got the idea from a friend who served on a Trident nuclear submarine. His friend said that in order to be an officer on one of these subs, you have to know how to do everyone else's job. Those skills are repeatedly trained and taught. In Phil's words,

> *"And I remember thinking, 'That's really cool.' So we implemented officer training at Evernote. The program is voluntary. If you sign up, we will randomly assign you to any other meeting. So pretty much anytime I have a meeting with anyone, or anyone else has a meeting with anyone, very often there is somebody else in there from a totally different department who's in officer training. They're there to absorb what we're talking about. They're not just spectators. They ask questions; they talk. My assistant runs it, and she won't schedule any individual for more than two extra meetings a week. We don't want this consuming too much of anybody's time."* {New York Times Endnote 311}

Chicago-based online advertising buyer **Centro LLC** (#155) focuses on the manager-employee relationship. Centro spends a lot of time training managers. Why? Because people quit bosses, not jobs. The biggest reason employees leave is because of their managers. Scott Golas, vice president of human resources says his company focuses on the manager-employee relationship,

> *"Let's face it: People leave companies because of their boss," Mr. Golas says. "We try to remove the typical obstacles (between bosses and employees) by sharing more information, by providing great training and by making sure those bosses have the right skill sets."* {Crain's Endnote 312}

A recent study by Assocham revealed,

> *"About 70% of [survey] respondents said that employees who quit their jobs complain about the indifferent attitude of their bosses or immediate supervisor."* {Endnote 313}

Want to increase employee engagement? It's not "rocket science." The single biggest driver {Forbes.com Endnote 314} is the quality of the relationship with the employee's direct manager. Put an emphasis on developing managers of people.

Gallup interviewed 10 million employees around the world. They asked them the following question,

> *"Would you agree with this statement, 'My supervisor or somebody at work, cares about me as a person?"*

Those who agreed were found to be,
1. More productive
2. Made greater contributions to profits
3. More likely to stay with the company long term {*The Happiness Advantage* Endnote 315}

Ecumen's (#316) *Velocity Leadership* program is another major way Ecumen honors and empowers achievement. Each year, up to 25 emerging leaders are selected for a very thought-provoking leadership development program that includes visits to other innovative companies to learn from them, guest speakers on innovation and leadership, and other learning and personal growth opportunities. It allows employees to step outside of their daily work and lives and focus on their personal growth as a person and leader. {Minneapolis / St. Paul Business Journal Endnote 316}

Squeeze In (#780), a group of California and Nevada restaurants, has an annual 3-day off-site management retreat called *Format*. According to Eva Lipson, "We get all our Managers and Owners together to review reports and numbers, discuss management styles, refresh our techniques, review our menu and hear suggestions to make it better, and most importantly bond and team build. We encourage self-development and management growth by offering up books to read (including your book: *What's Your Purple Goldfish*) and then we have them write short book reports. When they turn in their book reports, they get a cash bonus. This year we had a number of books on their list to read, and when they finished them all (and wrote reports on each), we presented them with free iPads! Also, during the 3-day retreat, we take them out to eat at restaurants (always interesting for a group of servers to go out and be served), and imbibe in a few cocktails too. We know that our *Format* retreat increases camaraderie, reinforces our company culture and helps with employee retention. It's a great way for us to show our Managers how much we love them and care about them, both professionally and personally." {Squeeze In Endnote 317}

TRAINING AS A COMPETITIVE DIFFERENTIATOR

Colliers founded Colliers University (CU) in 2002. It was truly a novel concept within the commercial real estate industry. Built on the premise that learning can be a competitive advantage, CU has grown to include more than 1,000 classes and has helped accelerate the professional and personal success of more than 7,000 Colliers professionals. The curriculum offers a 360-degree approach to learning with courses in commercial real estate, business and personal development. CU is not only a culture driver for the company internally; it is an outwardly competitive recruitment tool, raising the bar in terms of the expertise of their professionals. This expertise directly benefits clients through better results and memorable experiences." {Colliers Endnote 318}

MyLearning, the global online learning portal for **Accenture** (#237), boasts 20,000 learning courses that range from core training to technical training. Accenture Learning BPO Services and Accenture work together today to annually serve more than 125,000 learners through more than 200,000 classroom learning days and more than a 1,000 virtual learning sessions. The team discovered that for every dollar Accenture invests in learning, the company receives that dollar back plus an additional $3.53 in measurable value to their bottom line—in other words, a 353% return on learning. According to Jill Smart, Senior Managing Director of Human Resources at Accenture,

> *"Learning at Accenture is changing people's lives; it's giving them more reason than ever to stay with us and grow both personally and professionally."* {Atlanta Business Chronicle Endnote 319}

The Container Store (#460) puts an emphasis on training. Employees receive on an average 160+ hours of training per year. Typical annual turnover in retail is 100%, but at Container Store it hovers around 15-20%. {AchieveMax.com Endnote 320}

Wegman's (#507), a popular grocery store chain that started in upstate New York, trains their employees 2-3 more times than other grocery stores. In turn, turnover at the chain is only 7% compared to 19% industry-wide. {Jeanne Bliss Endnote 321}

TUITION REIMBURSEMENTS AND MORE

Hoar Construction (#56) puts an emphasis on personal and professional development. Employees receive up to $10,000 in annual tuition reimbursement, plus Hoar offers employees a variety of courses through their internal university ranging from money management and stress reduction, to tips on building a nonprofit. {Endnote 322}

Boeing (#327) pays for college degrees pertinent to position and provides stock awards for degree completion. {St. Louis Business Journal Endnote 323}

Monsanto (#481) encourages ongoing employee development with generous tuition subsidies (to $10,000), financial bonuses for course completion and subsidies for professional accreditation. {eluta.ca Endnote 324}

The Canadian crude and natural gas company **Nexen** (#668) invests in ongoing employee development through generous tuition subsidies to a maximum of $35,000. {eluta.ca Endnote 325}

STAYING CURIOUS AND CURRENT

Nina Hale (#284) strives to create a culture of curiosity and passion, even going out of its way to encourage employees to share information with each other. As part of that push, the company hosts weekly "shared education" meetings where an employee picks a topic to discuss. "There's a lot of new and different skill sets, so each person brings a new area of expertise to the table," Senior Account Manager Leslie Gibson said. "Everyone's willing to share what they've learned and no one ever makes anyone else feel stupid." {Minneapolis / St. Paul Business Journal Endnote 326}

One program at **Automation Direct** (#704) is called *Wake Up and Learn*. Between 8 and 9 a.m. four times a year, the company hosts a variety of speakers to discuss personal and professional development topics including budgeting, managing stress and healthy eating. {Entreprenuer.com Endnote 327}

Horizon Media (#747) has introduced the *Knowledge Café*, an educational series inviting media and tech executives to talk to employees and clients. Recent speakers include Hulu CEO Jason

Kilar and Pandora CEO Tim Westergren.

> *"We program our space in a way that's meaningful to employees. We're always trying to figure out how to stay current with the evolution of the business, but in a timeless way."* {Ad.Age.com Endnote 328}

VISUAL THINKING

Twice a month for two hours, employees at **XPLANE** (#709) meet to discuss various topics of personal and professional interest and to work on collaboration, storytelling and presentation skills. "The *Visual Learning School* is about using pictures to help people better think about complex issues, solve problems and communicate more effectively," says XPLANE creative director Matt Adams. "The most valued result is team building and the strengthening of relationships through learning, spontaneity and improvisation." {Endnote 329}

Training while Bouncing Around

There is one program at **Semco** (#787) that allows people to act like entrepreneurs at the company. According to CEO Ricardo Semler,

> *"Called 'Lost in Space', it assumes that young recruits don't know what they want to do with their lives. The program lets them roam the company for a year. They do what they want to do, move when they want to move, go where their interests take them; work for one, two, or six different units. At the end of the year, anyone they've worked for can offer them a job, or they can seek an opening in an area that interests them. If neither happens... we thank them for the year."* {*The Seven Day Weekend* Endnote 330}

LAGNIAPPE: SCUBA is an acronym for **S**elf **C**ontained **U**nderwater **B**reathing **A**pparatus. **Chesapeake Energy** (#78) provides employees with the opportunity to get certified for scuba diving for free. {The Daily Finance Endnote 331}

RETIREMENT

Let's look at a handful of companies that go the extra mile to prepare and take care of employees for life after work:

BIG CONTRIBUTIONS

Devon Energy (#206), a North American oil and gas explorer and producer, has developed a new 401(k) retirement plan that allows for annual company contributions between 11% to 22%. {Endnote 332}

GSM (#255), an IT consultancy in Leesburg, VA has big perks, including five weeks of vacation, a 401(k) contribution of 15% of salary, fully paid health-care premiums, $1,200 toward the creation of a will, $5,000 a year to attend training or conferences, $720 toward Internet access, and $1,750 toward the purchase of a gadget--although employees are given all the technology they need for their jobs. {Washingtonian Magazine Endnote 333}

PLANNING, PHASING, PREPARING

TD Bank (#449) helps employees plan for life after work with retirement planning assistance. The program includes a defined benefit pension plan, matching contributions to a share purchase plan, and a health benefits plan that extends into retirement with no age limit. {eluta.ca Endnote 334}

DIALOG (#468) is a multidisciplinary firm comprised of architects, engineers, interior designers, urban designers and planners. The firm helps older workers prepare for retirement with contributions to a matching RSP plan and phased-in work options that allow employees to gradually leave the workforce. {Endnote 335}

The **University of Toronto** (#493) offers a phased-in retirement work options for those nearing the end of their careers. They also help employees prepare for life after work with retirement planning assistance services along with generous contributions to a defined benefit pension plan. {eluta.ca Endnote 336}

British Columbia Safety Authority (#630) provides phased-in work options that allow employees to gradually leave the workforce and health benefit coverage that extends to retirees. {eluta.ca Endnote 337}

Chapter 19

GIVING BACK AND PAYING IT FORWARD

"From what we get, we can make a living;
what we give, however, makes a life."

- Arthur Ashe

The eighth inch on the 9 INCH journey to the heart of your employees involves **Paying it Forward**. Let's look at a Baker's Dozen of companies that go the *extra mile* to enable employees to serve those in need:

LETTING EMPLOYEES GIVE BACK

Umpqua Bank (#7) allows its employees to give back to the community. Here is a comment by employee Heather Primeaux, "We are given and encouraged to use 40 hours of paid time each year to volunteer, which I can and do use to volunteer at my kids' schools and for field trips." {money.cnn.com Endnote 338}

Volunteering is part of public relations firm **MWW**'s (#728) ethos. MWW created *Matter More Day* to give all employees the opportunity to volunteer for their favorite non-profit organization. On this day all offices close for one day of company-wide volunteering. Each year, the MWW Citizen of the Year Award is presented to one employee who has made an outstanding contribution to improving his or her community. The award includes a sizable donation made in his or her name to the charity of their choice. MWW programs include: *Tools for School* (MWW offices collect supplies for distribution to low-income and foster children); *Neighbor to Neighbor* (MWW kicks off the holiday season by helping food banks in its communities to obtain, prepare and distribute Thanksgiving meals for families in need); and *Letters to Santa*

(MWW makes wishes come true for hundreds of children in the communities in it works.) {PR News Online Endnote 339}

VOLUNTEERING PLUS A LITTLE EXTRA

Embrace Home Loans (#57) has the *Embrace Cares* program. The Newport based company offers 100 hours of paid time off per year for volunteering, and donates $10 for every hour worked by the employee to the volunteer organization of their choice. {GreatPlacetoWork.com Endnote 340}

Employees at **National Rural Electric Cooperative Association** (#261) are encouraged to volunteer. For every 24 hours of time an employee gives to charity, he or she receives an extra vacation day. {Washingtonian Magazine Endnote 341}

QBP (#414) gives $10 to any 501(c)3 organization for every hour its employees volunteer. Every employee can record up to 40 hours per year that QBP will pay out $10 per hour. Last year they logged 1,280 off-the-clock volunteer hours. This year they are shooting for 2,000. {Outside Magazine Endnote 342}

GIVING BACK AND DONATING

Microsoft (#276) donated $844 million worth of software to nearly 47,000 nonprofits in 2011. The Oregon office has an annual giving campaign where employee contributions are matched dollar-for-dollar. An added benefit, Microsoft gives the organizations $17 an hour for each hour of their employees' volunteer service. {Oregon Business Endnote 343}

TOMS Shoes (#44), without a doubt, will revolutionize how we look at corporate culture in the future. They are championing the idea [buy one, give one} that a company can sell a quality product, be profitable, and give back to those in need. {Quora.com Endnote 344}

Decision Analytics Corporation (#250), a military contractor, believes in giving back. Each quarter, staffers assemble care packages for soldiers overseas. {Washingtonian Magazine Endnote 345}

The employees of Canadian airline **WestJet** (#485) manage a highly focused charitable program called the *Community Investment Team,* which supports numerous initiatives and donates close to 5,000 flights to charitable initiatives each year. {eluta.ca Endnote 346}

LENDING SKILLS AS WELL AS HANDS

Hewlett Packard (#52) empowers employees to make a difference and give back. Let's do the math: 4 hours per month x 300,000 employees = 1,200,000 hours of HP social impact. {HP.com Endnote 347}

The Olympics are close to the heart of the people running and working for **Lane4** (#338). The company takes it name from the swimming lane given to the competitor with the fastest heat. The firm advises other businesses and human resources leaders on organizational change, leadership development and executive coaching. Adrian Moorhouse, who won swimming gold medal at the Seoul Games, set up Lane4 with a leading sports psychologist in 1995 to show that people can achieve excellence in everything they do if they have the right "high-performance" environment. They practice what they preach. The business contributes to the community in Bourne End, Buckinghamshire, running a free walk-in clinic on CV [resume] writing and interviewing techniques to help tackle local unemployment. {The Sunday Times Endnote 348}

SPONSORSHIP

Tabar (#412) fully sponsors a child in each full-time employee's name with the organization *Save the Children.* Tabar currently sponsors 23 children worldwide. Employees also get paid time off for approved volunteer work for community or church services. {Outside Magazine Endnote 349}

GOING ABOVE AND BEYOND

Knight Point Systems (#257), founded by a service-disabled veteran, has donated more than $106,000 to charity over the last three years. In addition, the management team buys lunches or dinners for service-members they see in airports. {Source: Washingtonian Magazine Endnote 350}

In 1986, **Patagonia** (#800) committed 1% of sales or 10% of pretax profits, whichever was greater, to local NGO's committed to fighting for the environment. In the last 26+ years the company has given tens of millions of dollars back to the environment. In addition, the outdoor-apparel maker (#188) also gives employees two weeks of full-paid leave to work for the green non-profit of their choice. {Inc.com Endnote 351}

Chapter 20

EMPOWERING DREAMS AND GOALS

"Life is work, and work is life, and both are a struggle.
It's doing meaningful workand being valued for
it--not picnics--that makes it all worthwhile."

- Vineet Nayar, CEO of HCL Technologies

The last inch on the 9 INCH journey to the heart of your employees is via **Empowerment**.

Leadership is about inspiring others. Enabling team members to do their absolute best to work towards a meaningful and rewarding shared purpose. In one word... EMPOWERMENT. Help people find their direction, support them with resources and then getting the hell out of the way.

Maybe one of the strongest examples of empowerment is **Nordstrom** (#34). Their entire mission and employee handbook fits on the back of a business card. Nordstrom has only one goal, "To provide outstanding customer service." They only have one rule, "Use good judgment in all situations." {Endnote 352}

IT'S TIME FOR A CHANGE

Command and Control or Carrot and Stick thinking is outdated. People do not enjoy or appreciate being controlled or coerced.

The best managers figure out how to get great outcomes by setting the appropriate context, rather than by trying to control their people. {Netflix, Reference Guide on our Freedom & Responsibility Culture Endnote 353}

According to noted leadership experts, Ken and Scott Blanchard,

"We are finding that giving people a chance to succeed in their job and setting them free to a certain degree is the key to motivation, as opposed to trying to direct and control people's energy. It's really about letting go and connecting people to their work--and each other--rather than channeling, organizing, orchestrating, and focusing behavior." {Fast Company Endnote 354}

Let's look at a **Baker's Dozen** of companies that go the *extra mile* to empower team members:

EMPOWERMENT IS THE OPPOSITE OF ORGANIZATION

W.L Gore (#46) was founded by Wilbert Lee Gore in 1958. A 16-year veteran at DuPont, Bill envisioned a different type of organization. His would be non-hierarchal, setting an environment where leader would emerge based on the merit of their ideas.

"[He] wanted a company where employees' spirit grew based on what they accomplished, not which corporate scrimmage they had won—where more time was spent generating ideas than generating ways to cover one's backside. So he decided to create a 'non-organization' approach for his new company that would inspire creativity in its employees." {Jeanne Bliss Endnote 355}

Life Coaches and Dream Managers

Zappos (#72) provides a life coach for employees. {YouTube Endnote 356}

Inspired by Matthew Kelly's book, *The Dream Manager*, **Infusionsoft** (#455) provides employees with the services of a "Dream Manager." Dreaming is a core value at Infusionsoft. The sales and marketing automation provider believes in people and their dreams. The Dream Manager works to help team members set, pursue and become accountable for achieving their goals and dreams. {Infusionsoft Endnote 357}

The commercial developer **Brasfield & Gorrie** (#239) created a new position, Director of Career Development. The move is paying dividends. The company maps out each employee's career path, and indicates what he or she will have to do to get there. "Every employee's career path is consistent with what we're looking for from our strategic plan five to 10 years out. We're not just making something up." Spelling out every employee's career path takes time and part of that time is spent making sure upper management communicates the results with individual employees. {Atlanta Business Chronicle Endnote 358}

SUPPORTING PERSONAL GOALS

Associates at **Pepsico** (#537) include a personal goal in their performance development review process and are asked to deliver against this goal, just like any other goal, to ensure a work-life balance. {BusinessInsider.com Endnote 359}

Following the opportunity to take time to evaluate where the associate is now, and where he or she wants to be, each team member at **Fahlgren Mortine** (#725) then meets with his or her supervisor for a conversation; at least one hour devoted to focusing on the individual's needs and goals, and a chance to formally discuss ways he or she can grow and learn in the development of his or her career. {PR News Online Endnote 360}

TITLES NEED NOT APPLY

This leading developer empowers everyone to make a personal mark on the company and culture. According to Mike Derheim, CEO at **The Nerdery** (#304),

> *We want them to aspire to be a co-president. The late great Luke Bucklin was the only president we'll ever have, and co-president was what he called us — all of us — before we lost him. In one of Luke's last all-staff e-mails he wrote: "Put your business card on the desk in front of you. Look at it. ... This*

*card does not define you. You are a **Co-President**. You are bigger than your defined role. ... Play your part — transcend your job title, be a hero." (Source: Minneapolis / St. Paul Business Journal)* {Endnote 361}

According to Matt DeGeronimo at **Smith Floyd** (#771), "I run a mergers & acquisitions company in Honolulu, and had some thoughts for your book. There is one thing we do that might not be commonplace. We allow employees to pick their own title. Creative titles are encouraged." {Endnote 362}

The independent marketing agency **WONGDOODY** (#215) is united by the *Democracy of Good Ideas* principle. Any staffer could come up with the next big idea. It encourages participation and rewards keen judgment. {Los Angeles Business Journal Endnote 363}

PURPOSEFULLY LOSING CONTROL

One of Europe's leading manufacturers and suppliers of single-use medical products, **Molnlycke Health Care** (#61) allowed production teams to decide how to meet their goals. With the responsibility for quality products moved to individuals on those teams, nearly 70% of the company's new products launch on time, compared with just 15% previously. As a result, the company will have quadrupled its shareholder value in only five years. {InnoSupport Endnote 364}

PASSIONS AND THE CREATIVE MUSE

Fast Horse (#297) is an innovative, integrated agency offering a full range of traditional and non-traditional marketing services. Fast Horse employees enjoy little extras like *Muse It or Lose It*, a $500 stipend to help underwrite creative endeavors away from the office. {Endnote 365}

Much of the credit for creating an amazing workplace at **Weber Shandwick Minneapolis** (#310) goes to their *Employee Action Group* (EAG). Each month, employees enjoy an EAG-sponsored event to celebrate our successes, encourage teamwork or to just have fun. The highlight events include the annual *"Shank-wick"* golf outing and a version of "The Amazing Race," appropriately renamed *"The Shan-mazing Race."* Weber's newest EAG initiative is the *"No Boundaries"* program. This program was designed to give employees a chance to explore a personal passion, which may include attending "The Burning Man" event in San Francisco to spark creativity, or traveling to Honduras to work for *Soles4Souls*, a nonprofit organization devoted to distributing shoes and clothing to victims of abject suffering. The company provides the employees with five extra vacation days and $1,000 to pursue the passion. {Minneapolis / St. Paul Business Journal Endnote 366}

MAKING TIME FOR EMPOWERMENT

3M (#53) launched the 15% program in 1948. Employees were given 15% of their time to work on personal project of their choosing. If it seems radical now, imagine how it played as post-war America was suiting up and going to the office, with rigid hierarchies and increasingly defined work and home roles. But it was also a logical next step. Fifteen percent time is extended to everyone. Who knows who'll create the next *Post-It Note?* (a 15% time innovation)

> *"It's one of the things that sets 3M apart as an innovative company, by sticking to that culture of giving every one of our employees the ability to follow their instincts to take advantage of opportunities for the company," says Technical Director Kurt Beinlich, who tries to get most of his 70-person lab team to participate.* {Endnote 367}

TAKEAWAY: Forty plus years in the red taught 3M a key lesson: *Innovate or Die*, an ethos the company has carried dutifully into the 21st century.

Azavea (#187), a maker of mapping software, lets employees spend up to 10% of their time on research projects of their own devising. {Inc.com Endnote 368}

HACK DAYS AND THE QUEST FOR IMPROVEMENT

Conductor, Inc. (#513) holds an annual, companywide Hack Day, where all Conductors are invited to self-organize into teams and spend a day developing an idea that makes the product, office or company better. {GreatPlacetoWork.com Endnote 369}

Siemens (#606) operates an employee suggestion program that encourages employees to share their feedback -- the ideas that lead to savings or new revenues are evaluated for their impact and can lead to financial bonus payments ranging up to $100,000. {Endnote 370}

Employees at **McMurry** (#706) can submit their innovative *WOW Project* ideas through the company's internal computer network. Toward the end of the year, president and CEO Chris McMurry and several senior managers consider each of the hundreds of pitches that come in and award up to $10,000 for the best ideas. "Our business, and every business, needs to innovate constantly if it seeks an enduring future," McMurry says, explaining why the program got started. One winning pitch came from a group of three employees who poured over U.S. Post Office regulations and came up with a way for McMurry to re-sequence how it distributes mail on behalf of its clients, saving those clients millions of dollars.

Encouraging its staff of more than 170 people to dream up creative business ideas and solutions has cemented innovation into our culture," McMurry says. "It's now part of what everyone does. It has put all my colleagues in a continuous improvement mode. There literally isn't a week that goes by where someone doesn't implement a better way of doing something."

McMurry says *WOW Projects* improve a swath of company functions, from billing accuracy to workflow to shipping procedures. All have improved the company's bottom line. {Entrepreneur.com Endnote 371}

R&D THURSDAY'S

Nearly every employee at **Spider Strategies** (#268) works from home every day and vacation is unlimited. Staffers set their own hours--which suits those who prefer to work at night. There are rarely meetings--three or four a year. Every Thursday is set-aside for R&D, so staffers can explore the latest in technology. {Washingtonian Magazine Endnote 372}

THE ABILITY TO CORRECT MISTAKES

Starbucks (#520) will fix your drink if it's wrong, every time – no charge. Starbucks employees are empowered to provide drinks on the house for repeat customers when they are having a bad day, out of money or "just because". Crewmembers spend a day during their first week of training simply going out into the lobby and greeting customers. The goal is not just to ask them what they need or if they can provide a refill, but to actually engage in conversation and help the person become more comfortable while waiting or relaxing. Crewmembers are empowered to provide "service recovery certificates" for a free "anything" (even a quad-venti 5 pump caramel macchiato, light whip, hold the foam) when service fails to meet the customer's expectations. {Jordan Belcher Endnote 373}

Tellers at **Fairwinds Credit Union** (#522) are empowered to provide immediate service recovery of up to $100 per incident without seeking management approval. This can be used to buy a customer lunch, purchase flowers, send a special treat or for anything else the employee decides to help recover from a bad service experience. {Endnote 374}

EXHIBITION AND SCIENCE FAIRS

Practice Plan (#377), which provides business support services to the dental sector, gets the creative juices flowing among its workforce of 74 people by giving in-house exhibition space for original artwork every two months. Darren Marks used his turn to show a series of nine images called Words To Live Your Life By, based on song lyrics. Colleagues shared drinks and nibbles at the opening of his *"Wall 9"* exhibition. {Endnote 375}

Bazaarvoice (#409) makes sure it solicits the views of its own people, too, and holds a science fair to showcase bright ideas. (Source: The Sunday Times Endnote 376}

Once a year, about 200 employees from dozens of divisions at **3M** (#857) make cardboard posters describing their 15% time project as if they were presenting volcano models at a middle school science fair. They stand up their poster and then hang out next to it. There they await feedback, suggestions, and potential co-collaborators. Wayne Maurer is an R&D manager in 3M's abrasives division and calls it a chance for people to unhinge their "inner geek." He elaborates: "For technical people, it's the most passionate and engaged event we have at 3M." {FastDesignCo. Endnote 377}

FINAL THOUGHTS

I hope you enjoyed the book. Here are five final points about green goldfish:

You Can't Make Chicken Salad...

You can't make chicken salad out of chicken poop [apologies for using "poop" as I have a five and a seven year old]. Creating green goldfish is not a substitute for having a strong product or service. Hire the right people, compensate them fairly and allow them to do meaningful work. Get the basics right before giving the little unexpected extras.

Authentic vs. Forced

A green goldfish is a beacon. It's a small gift or benefit that demonstrates you care. Why do we love our parents? It's because they loved us first. Green Goldfish need to be given in an authentic way. If it comes across as forced or contrived, you'll eliminate all of the goodwill and negatively impact your culture.

A Daily Regiment of Exercise vs. Liposuction

A green goldfish is not a quick fix or for those seeking immediate results. Translation: it's not liposuction. It's equivalent to working out everyday. Culture gradually builds and improves over time.

It's a Commitment, Not a Campaign

A green goldfish is different than a one off or limited offer. Add one or a school of green goldfish at your convenience, remove them at your peril [did someone just say TOWELS?].

Every Great Journey Begins With a Single Step

Start small when adding a signature extra and add gradually. Remember the concept of Trojan Mice. The best brands are those who boast a whole school of green goldfish.

ADDITIONAL INSPIRATION & FURTHER READING

Looking for companies that embrace green goldfish strategy?

Here's the inaugural Green Goldfish Hall of Fame:

Class of 2013
> Semco
> Google
> SAS Institute
> Clif Bar
> Evernote
> Zappos
> McMurry
> Patagonia
> HCL Technologies
> Coyne PR
> Starbucks

Recommended Reading:

What's Your Purple Goldfish? 12 Ways to Win Customers and Influence WoM – Stan Phelps

Employee First, Customers Second - Vineet Nayar

Drive: The Surprising Truth About What Motivates Us - Daniel Pink

Let My People Go Surfing, The Education of a Reluctant Businessman - Yvon Choinard

Delivering Happiness: A Path to Profits, Passion, and Purpose - Tony Hsieh

Influence - Robert Cialdini

Peak: How Great Companies Get Their Mojo from Maslow - Chip Conley

Dream Manager - Matthew Kelly and Patrick Lencioni

Maverick: The Success Story Behind the World's Most Unusual Workplace - Ricardo Semler

The Seven Day Weekend - Ricardo Semler

Touchpoints - Doug Conant

Why Works Sucks & How to Fix It: No Schedules, No Meetings, No Joke - Ressler, Thompson

Ownership Quotient - James L. Heskett, W. Earl Sasser, Joe Wheeler

Uncommon Service - Frances Frei and Anne Morriss

ABOUT THE AUTHOR

Stan Phelps is an "experience architect", author, professor and popular keynote speaker. He believes that marketing must focus on differentiation to win the hearts of both employees and customers. Stan motivates audiences with his insatiable desire to create meaningful change in marketing. Having collected over 2,000 examples of purple and green goldfish, he's fluent in illustrating complex business concepts, communicating in ways that resonate, provoking creative thought and innovation.

What's Your Purple Goldfish was the first book in a trilogy on the subject. This book is the second installment focused on employees. The final book, *What's Your Golden Goldfish* will take a look a the signature extras a business provides to the top 20% of customers and top 20% of employees.

Stan received a BS in marketing from Marist College and a JD/MBA from Villanova University. He lives in Cary, North Carolina with his wife Jennifer, their two boys Thomas & James, a Glen of Imaal Terrier named MacMurphy and a rescued black cat named Rudy.

Driven by client objectives and inspired by bold vision, Stan works with clients to create keynotes, breakout sessions and workshops that are memorable and on brand, inspiring businesses to become talkable by design.

The result: programs that win BIG.

Twitter: @9inchmarketing
Facebook: facebook.com/9inchmarketing
Email: stan@9inchmarketing.com
Website: 9inchmarketing.com
Phone: +1.919.360.4702

Endnotes

1. http://hr.toolbox.com/blogs/employee-engagement-leadership/chain-of-connection-leaders-gt-employees-gt-customers-37611
2. http://www.danpink.com/drive
3. http://careerbliss.com/
4. http://bits.blogs.nytimes.com/2012/10/17/larry-page-on-regulation-maps-and-googles-social-mission/
5. http://googlepress.blogspot.com/2009/05/larry-pages-university-of-michigan.html
6. http://www.seattlepi.com/business/article/Grumbling-at-Microsoft-grows-1145655.php
7. http://minimsft.blogspot.com/2006/05/microsofts-may-18th-2006-big-turning.html
8. http://www.businessweek.com/stories/2005-09-25/troubling-exits-at-microsoft
9. http://www.gallup.com/poll/150383/majority-american-workers-not-engaged-jobs.aspx
10. http://www.theworkfoundation.com/Reports
11. http://www.accenture.com/SiteCollectionDocuments/PDF/harnessing.pdf
12. http://www.slideshare.net/businessandthegeek/human-resources-employee-engagement-statistics
13. http://www.slideshare.net/businessandthegeek/human-resources-employee-engagement-statistics
14. http://www.hci.org/blog/we-re-engaged
15. http://www.asaecenter.org/Resources/EUArticle.cfm?ItemNumber=11514
16. http://www.thesocialworkplace.com/2011/08/08/social-knows-employee-engagement-statistics-august-2011-edition/
17. http://rapidbi.com/howtowriteaninternalcommunicationsplanandstrategy/
18. http://accenture.com/
19. http://www.bain.com/about/people-and-values/our-team/profiles/chris-zook.aspx
20. http://www.towerswatson.com/
21. http://www.gallup.com/home.aspx
22. http://www.towerswatson.com/
23. http://www.hcltech.com/
24. http://www.dailymail.co.uk/travel/article-1356550/Amsterdam-city-break-Travel-Holland-s-historic-city-canals-capital.html#ixzz2H0yb1ufa
25. http://www.coynepr.com/pdf/bestagency.pdf
26. http://switchandshift.com/lead-like-all-your-employees-are-volunteers
27. http://www.youtube.com/watch?v=CQ71xcOX_qA
28. http://www.novareinna.com/festive/mardi.html
29. https://www.mckinseyquarterly.com/Organization/Talent/Motivating_people_Getting_beyond_money_2460#footnote1
30. http://www.entrepreneur.com/topic/motivation
31. http://www.talentinnovation.org/
32. file://localhost/Sylvia%20Ann%20Hewlett%20http/::blogs.hbr.org:hbr:hewlett:2012:05:attract_and_keep_a-players_wit.html
33. http://www.merriam-webster.com/dictionary/lagniappe
34. http://www.gutenberg.org/files/245/245-h/245-h.htm
35. http://en.wikipedia.org/wiki/Assize_of_Bread_and_Ale
36. http://www.trojanmice.com/index.htm
37. http://en.wikipedia.org/wiki/Gift_economy
38. http://socialmediamediasres.wordpress.com/2011/02/16/social-media-is-like-beer-buying-the-gift-economy-in-social-media/

39. http://www.chicagobusiness.com/article/20120331/ISSUE02/120329728/why-your-perks-arent-working#ixzz2GTJCduld
40. http://adage.com/article/cmo-strategy/marketing-effective-word-mouth-disrupts-schemas/141734/
41. http://books.google.com/books/about/The_Seven_Day_Weekend.html?id=JytCGVpFOEYC
42. http://www.semco.com.br/en/content.asp?content=4&contentID=580
43. http://www.daredevilrun.com/
44. http://www.etana.co.za/content/page/the-etana-academy/
45. http://www.etana.co.za/news/entry/etana-redwards-winners-2013
46. http://www.etana.co.za/content/page/business-brand
47. http://list.ly/list/1Ni-purple-goldfish-project
48. http://www.youtube.com/watch?feature=player_embedded&v=QWKthxnNCWk
49. http://claytonfletcher.com/bio.cfm
50. http://www.peppercomm.com/our_pov/why-stand-up-comedy-is-good-for-your-business
51. http://peppercomm.com/about/
52. http://www.crainsnewyork.com/features/best-places-to-work
53. http://www.flickr.com/photos/puliarfanita/5163796247/
54. http://www.forbes.com/sites/meghancasserly/2012/08/08/heres-what-happens-to-google-employees-when-they-die/
55. http://goodthinkinc.com/
56. http://list.ly/list/1OE-green-goldfish-project
57. http://computer.howstuffworks.com/googleplex2.htm
58. http://www.huffingtonpost.com/2012/01/30/google-benefits-employee-perks_n_1242707.html#s649145&title=Japanese_Toto_Toilets
59. http://www.huffingtonpost.com/2012/01/30/google-benefits-employee-perks_n_1242707.html#s649180&title=Endless_Lap_Pools
60. http://mashable.com/2010/07/01/google-lgbt-health/
61. http://www.forbes.com/sites/meghancasserly/2012/08/08/heres-what-happens-to-google-employees-when-they-die/
62. http://www.businessinsider.com/marissa-mayer-tip-on-preventing-employee-burn-out-2012-9#ixzz26OsA6vK2
63. http://www.pcmag.com/slideshow_viewer/0,3253,l=238614&a=238614&po=1,00.asp
64. file://localhost/source/%20http/::www.mercurynews.com:business:ci_17162973
65. http://resources.greatplacetowork.com/article/pdf/why_google_is_no._1.pdf
66. http://www.businessinsider.com/the-25-best-places-to-work-around-the-world-2012-11?op=1#ixzz2E91MDTvv
67. http://computer.howstuffworks.com/googleplex.htm
68. https://developers.google.com/chart/image/docs/gallery/googleometer_chart#introduction
69. http://www.entrepreneur.com/article/219509
70. http://www.9inchmarketing.com/2012/10/31/the-power-of-marketing-g-l-u-e/
71. http://www.inc.com/winning-workplaces/articles/201105/employee-onboarding-done-better.html
72. http://en.wikipedia.org/wiki/Onboarding
73. http://www.inc.com/winning-workplaces/articles/201105/employee-onboarding-done-better.html
74. https://www1.umn.edu/ohr/prod/groups/ohr/@pub/@ohr/@toolkit/documents/asset/ohr_asset_175051.pdf

75. http://www.businessinsider.com/companies-with-awesome-perks-2012-10?op=1
76. http://www.businessinsider.com/
77. http://boss.blogs.nytimes.com/2013/03/13/getting-employees-off-to-a-good-start/
78. http://blog.asana.com/2013/02/onboarding-new-engineers/
79. http://www.tampabay.com/news/business/workinglife/capital-ones-open-culture-helps-make-it-one-of-tampa-bays-top-workplaces/1227026
80. http://www.businessinsider.com/the-25-best-places-to-work-around-the-world-2012-11?op=1
81. http://www.netpromoter.com/netpromoter_community/blogs/jeanne_bliss/2011/12/13/usaa-grows-promoters-by-walking-in-their-customers-shoes
82. http://www.fastcompany.com/3004701/want-motivated-employees-put-them-contact-people-they-help
83. http://www.hbs.edu/faculty/Pages/profile.aspx?facId=6409
84. http://www.greatplacetowork.com/2012-best-workplaces/customink
85. http://blog.hulu.com/2011/06/13/working-in-the-future/
86. http://entreprenuer.com/
87. http://www.rotman.utoronto.ca/ProfessionalDevelopment/InitiativeForWomenInBusiness/Programs/Back%20to%20Work%20Program.aspx
88. http://www.prnewsonline.com/awards/top-work-places/2012/11/29/2012-top-places-to-work-in-pr-davies/
89. http://www.inc.com/winning-workplaces/articles/201105/employee-onboarding-done-better.html
90. http://www.inc.com/winning-workplaces/201105/box-net.html
91. http://blogs.hbr.org/taylor/2008/05/why_zappos_pays_new_employees.html
92. http://www.zapposinsights.com/about/faqs
93. http://www.sas.com/company/about/history.html#s1=3
94. http://webspace.ship.edu/nwgoates/OB/wharton_worklife_case--sas.pdf
95. http://www.fastcompany.com/
96. http://wraltechwire.com/business/tech_wire/news/blogpost/8979384/
97. http://www.inc.com/ss/2011-inc-5000-sas-jim-goodnight-corporate-shangri-la.html
98. http://www.inc.com/ss/2011-inc-5000-sas-jim-goodnight-corporate-shangri-la.html
99. http://www.onedayonejob.com/jobs/ryan-partnership/
100. http://rebelutionary.blogs.atlassian.com/2007/03/life_is_a_hire_way_5_tips_for_startup_hi.html
101. http://www.greatplacetowork.com/2012-best-workplaces/cirrus-logic
102. http://www.boston.com/jobs/news/articles/2011/11/06/employee_perks_hubspot_has_free_beer/
103. http://blog.nwjobs.com/peoples_picks_2010/large_company/most_unusual_perks_1.html
104. http://blog.nwjobs.com/peoples_picks_2010/small_company/coolest_office_space.html?lid=710013
105. http://www.businessinsider.com/the-best-perks-in-tech-2012-7?op=1#ixzz23WHRnqpZ
106. http://mashable.com/2012/05/28/startup-perks-culture/?utm_medium=email&utm_source=newsletter
107. www.chicagobusiness.com/article/20110402/ISSUE02/304029994/best-places-to-work-no-14-digitas-inc#ixzz23eYCahfV
108. http://www.businessinsider.com/companies-with-awesome-perks-2012-10?op=1#ixzz2EBoyA9J1
109. http://outsideonline.com

110. http://www.prnewsonline.com/awards/top-work-places/2012/11/29/2012-top-places-to-work-in-pr-lippe-taylor-brand-communications/
111. http://www.nytimes.com/2012/10/20/us/in-silicon-valley-perks-now-begin-at-home.html?pagewanted=all&_r=1&
112. http://www.bluebuddhaboutique.com/b3/about/
113. http://www.forbes.com/sites/markfidelman/2012/05/24/microsofts-view-of-the-future-workplace-is-brilliant-heres-why-2/2/
114. http://www.youtube.com/watch?feature=player_embedded&v=fomHaegp-4o
115. http://www.gyro.com/
116. http://www.interiorarchitects.com/
117. http://www.forbes.com/sites/georgebradt/2012/08/07/steelcase-ceo-on-how-office-layout-impacts-corporate-culture/
118. http://www.inc.com/magazine/20100201/the-way-i-work-paul-english-of-kayak_pagen_2.html
119. http://www.bizjournals.com/atlanta/
120. http://adage.com/article/best-places-to-work/places-work-media-marketing-bgt-partners/229314/
121. http://www.bizjournals.com/twincities/print-edition/2011/08/19/fast-horse-inc.html?page=all
122. http://www.tdcanadatrust.com/easyweb5/crr-2011/workplace/health_safety/index.jsp
123. http://www.cult-branding.com/business-life/articles-on-business-life/mindfulness-in-the-workplace/
124. http://www.boston.com/jobs/news/articles/2011/11/06/partners__simons_has_cell_phone_booths_for_privacy/
125. http://www.bizjournals.com/stlouis/
126. http://www.thesundaytimes.co.uk/sto/
127. http://www.businessinsider.com/the-25-best-small-companies-to-work-for-right-now-2012-10?op=1#ixzz2E945CFga
128. http://www.bizjournals.com/twincities/print-edition/2011/08/19/clockwork-active-media-systems.html?page=all
129. http://www.stlmag.com/St-Louis-Magazine/January-2009/Great-Places-to-Work/index.php?cparticle=2&siarticle=1
130. http://www.9inchmarketing.com/2013/01/18/beyond-dilbert-the-importance-of-design-in-the-workplace-for-employee-engagement/
131. http://www.entrepreneur.com/article/220512
132. http://www.cbsnews.com/8301-505263_162-57451292/huffington-talks-sleep-overbooked-huffpost-nap-rooms/?tag=showDoorFlexGridRight;flexGridModule
133. http://www.worldatwork.org/waw/adimComment?id=58501
134. http://money.cnn.com/magazines/fortune/bestcompanies/2011/snapshots/25.html
135. http://www.chron.com/business/top-workplaces/article/Paid-volunteer-time-dogs-at-work-and-other-perks-2254147.php
136. http://www.forbes.com/sites/karlmoore/2012/05/14/employees-first-customers-second-why-it-really-works-in-the-market/
137. http://www.icmrindia.org/casestudies/catalogue/Human%20Resource%20and%20Organization%20Behavior/Semco-A%20Maverick%20Organization-Human%20Resource%20Management.htm
138. http://www.knowledgeforaction.info/articolo.php?id=57
139. http://www.fastcompany.com/32710/you-have-no-boss
140. http://adage.com/article/special-report-best-places-to-work-2012/ad-age-s-places-work-11-marina-maher-communication/233647/

141. http://atlassian.com/
142. http://www.careercast.com/career-news/keys-great-corporate-culture-improving-employee-engagement
143. http://www.bizjournals.com/twincities/print-edition/2011/08/19/catalyst-studios-inc.html?page=all
144. http://www.satmetrix.com/symantecs-customer-champion-uses-customer-feedback-to-drive-business-results/
145. http://www.boston.com/jobs/news/articles/2011/11/06/the_best_employers_appreciate_their_workers/
146. www.labusinessjournal.com/
147. http://www.greatplacetowork.com/storage/documents/publications/top-ten-people-practices.pdf
148. http://adage.com/article/special-report-best-places-to-work-2012/team-12-ad-age-s-places-work-list/233662/
149. http://www.youtube.com/watch?v=aJ_2255KqoE
150. http://www.prnewsonline.com/
151. http://features.thesundaytimes.co.uk/public/best100companies/live/template
152. http://www.glassdoor.com/index.htm
153. http://bizjournals/twincities
154. http://hbswk.hbs.edu/item/5917.html
155. http://www.chicagorealestatedaily.com/article/20110402/ISSUE02/304029982/best-places-to-work-no-20-belvedere-trading-llc#ixzz23ecI6mZ6
156. http://www.chron.com/
157. http://publix.com/
158. http://bizjournals/twincities
159. http://features.thesundaytimes.co.uk/public/best100companies/live/template
160. http://features.thesundaytimes.co.uk/public/best100companies/live/template
161. http://www.semco.com.br/en/content.asp?content=4&contentID=570
162. http://www.dailyfinance.com/2010/12/22/successful-companies-gain-profits-by-adding-employee-benefits/
163. http://www.qwqhc.ca/knowledge-exchange-archived-05.aspx
164. http://www.greatplacetowork.net/publications-and-events/blogs-and-news/547
165. http://www.prnewsonline.com/awards/top-work-places/2012/11/29/2012-top-places-to-work-in-pr-borshoff/
166. http://www.intelihealth.com/IH/ihtPrint/EMIHC267/333/29758/1471698.html?hide=t&k=basePrint
167. www.thesundaytimes.co.uk/
168. http://corporate.reebok.com/en/about_reebok/Reebok CrossFit.asp
169. http://www.eluta.ca/top-employer-accenture
170. http://www.eluta.ca
171. http://www.outsideonline.com/
172. http://www.gentlegiant.com/Moving-Companies.aspx
173. http://www.chicagobusiness.com/article/20110402/ISSUE02/304029983/best-places-to-work-no-19-alterian-inc#ixzz23ec6nxuQ
174. http://assets.starbucks.com/assets/7343fbbdc87845ff9a000ee009707893.pdf
175. http://www.outsideonline.com/magazine
176. http://www.outsideonline.com/magazine
177. www.labusinessjournal.com
178. www.bizjournals.com/stlouis/

179. http://www.libertymutualgroup.com/omapps/ContentServer?pagename=LMGroup/Views/LMG&ft=4&fid=1138356724752
180. http://dixonschwabl.com/news/dixon-schwabl-ranked-19th-great-place-work-list
181. http://adage.com/article/special-report-best-places-to-work-2012/bgt-partners-15-ad-age-s-places-work-list/233657/
182. http://www.cbjonline.com/a2labj/supplements/BestPlaceToWork_1208.pdf
183. http://www.tedrubin.com/the-new-employee-wellness-and-social-connection-plan-powered-by-nikefuel/
184. http://www.amazon.com/Make-Their-Day-Employee-Recognition/dp/1620640546
185. http://www.wholeliving.com/133935/best-company-perks
186. http://GreatPlacetoWork.com/publications-and-events/blogs-and-news/1613-employee-well-being
187. http://news.yahoo.com/blogs/abc-blogs/boss-gives-employees-7-500-vacations-143431561--abc-news-topstories.html
188. http://www.nytimes.com/2012/04/08/business/phil-libin-of-evernote-on-its-unusual-corporate-culture.html?pagewanted=1&_r=3&
189. http://www.newbelgium.com/brewery/company/benefits.aspx
190. http://www.washingtonian.com/articles/work-education/50-great-places-to-work-in-washington/
191. http://features.thesundaytimes.co.uk/public/best100companies/live/template
192. http://element212.com/
193. http://www.theglobeandmail.com/report-on-business/careers/career-advice/four-unique-employee-benefits-youve-never-heard-of/article4620730/
194. http://www.prnewsonline.com/awards/top-work-places/2012/11/29/2012-top-places-to-work-in-pr-bain-company/
195. http://www.eluta.ca/top-employer-bank-of-canada
196. http://www.eluta.ca/top-employer-canadian-security-intelligence-service
197. http://www.crainsnewyork.com/gallery/20091207/FEATURES/120209998/9#ixzz1zQopu8qb
198. file:///localhost/source/%20http/::www.salary.com:14-companies-with-incredible-employee-perks
199. http://www.youtube.com/watch?v=MNuOmTQdFjA
200. http://www.dailyfinance.com/2011/08/24/companies-that-treat-workers-right-get-good-karma-right-back/
201. http://www.chicagobusiness.com/article/20120331/ISSUE02/120329728/why-your-perks-arent-working#ixzz2GTIIxYjc
202. http://www.thecareerrevolution.com/2008/03/most-unusual-company-perksscuba-diving.html
203. http://www.outsideonline.com/outdoor-adventure/best-jobs/The-30-Best-Places-to-Work-Strava-20120726.html
204. http://www.cbjonline.com/a2labj/supplements/BestPlaceToWork_1208.pdf
205. http://www.washingtonian.com/articles/work-education/great-places-to-work-healthy-glow/
206. http://www.nytimes.com/2012/10/20/us/in-silicon-valley-perks-now-begin-at-home.html?pagewanted=all&_r=2&
207. http://news.walgreens.com/article_print.cfm?article_id=5653
208. http://www.salary.com/14-companies-with-incredible-employee-perks
209. http://www.davethomasfoundation.org/

210. http://benefits.carmax.com/files/2013%20Adoption%20Assistance%20Policy.pdf
211. http://www.alston.com/careers-law-students-benefits/
212. http://www.customerthink.com/blog/a_newborn_bonus_is_literally_a_little_extra_facebook
213. https://www.businessgrouphealth.org/pub/f3002033-2354-d714-51d4-f144c4d536e8
214. http://www.eluta.ca/work-at-university-of-alberta
215. http://blog.brazencareerist.com/2012/04/17/amazingly-attractive-perks-that-will-have-you-drooling-over-employers/
216. http://www.greatplacetowork.net/publications-and-events/blogs-and-news/1496
217. http://www.glassdoor.com/Reviews/Employee-Review-T-Mobile-RVW183172.htm
218. http://www.businessinsider.com/the-25-best-small-companies-to-work-for-right-now-2012-10?op=1#ixzz2E9AzZa51
219. http://m.businessknowhow.com/manage/beatings.htm
220. http://www.eluta.ca/top-employer-xe-dot-com
221. http://www.aboutone.com/about-us/job-opportunities/comeback-mom-returnships/
222. http://money.cnn.com/magazines/fortune/bestcompanies/snapshots/2102.html
223. http://features.thesundaytimes.co.uk/public/best100companies/live/template
224. http://www.businessinsider.com/the-25-best-small-companies-to-work-for-right-now-2012-10?op=1#ixzz2E9DcIGH5
225. http://www.bizjournals.com/twincities/news/2011/08/19/best-places-to-work-rankings.html?page=all
226. http://www.chron.com/news/article/No-1-large-company-Anadarko-Petroleum-Corp-4021031.php
227. http://www.bizjournals.com/twincities/news/2011/08/19/best-places-to-work-rankings.html?page=all
228. http://www.chron.com/business/article/At-Hospice-Compassus-an-emotional-job-to-do-and-2252843.php
229. http://www.bizjournals.com/twincities/news/2011/08/19/best-places-to-work-rankings.html?page=all
230. http://www.eluta.ca/top-employer-cameco
231. http://www.greatplacetowork.com/2012-best-workplaces/customink
232. http://www.chicagobusiness.com/article/20120331/ISSUE02/120329728/why-your-perks-arent-working#ixzz2GTKHz2Hm
233. http://www.boston.com/jobs/news/articles/2011/11/06/employee_perks_harmonix_offers_band_practice_space/
234. http://adage.com/article/best-places-to-work/places-work-media-marketing-ubermind/229311/
235. http://www.entrepreneur.com/article/220512
236. http://www.bizjournals.com/twincities/print-edition/2011/08/19/zeus-jones-ltd.html?page=all
237. http://money.cnn.com/gallery/news/companies/2013/01/17/best-companies-perks.fortune/11.html
238. http://www.eluta.ca/top-employer-pricewaterhousecoopers
239. http://www.brw.com.au/p/sections/features/obs_takes_it_on_trust_VRWD3jsr3gF2zw1yGjqJwO
240. http://www.tribeinc.com/pdfs/SupplierGlobalResource_050109.pdf
241. http://www.coynepr.com/working_at_coyne.html

242. http://www.supplierglobalresource-digital.com/article/SALES+%26+MARKETING%3A+STRATEGIES+FOR+TODAY'S+SUPPLIERS/151001/0/article.html
243. http://www.worldatwork.org/waw/adimComment?id=58501
244. http://mashable.com/2011/08/07/startup-employee-perks/
245. http://adage.com/article/best-places-to-work/places-work-media-marketing-allen-gerritsen/229313/
246. http://www.angelamaiers.com/2011/08/new-ted-talk-you-matter.html
247. http://www.amazon.com/How-Win-Friends-Influence-People/dp/0671027034
248. http://accountemps.rhi.mediaroom.com/index.php?s=189&item=213
249. http://goodthinkinc.com/the-happiness-advantage/
250. http://www.bizjournals.com/twincities/print-edition/2011/08/19/the-nerdery.html?page=all
251. http://www.bizjournals.com/twincities/print-edition/2011/08/19/labreche.html?page=all
252. http://www.linkedin.com/pub/michael-poulsen/0/41/421
253. http://www.youtube.com/watch?v=iOxGVJ3Zv94
254. http://myragolden.wordpress.com/2009/04/21/how-being-gumby-can-transform-your-service-culture/
255. http://www.entrepreneur.com/gptw/75
256. http://www.youtube.com/watch?v=q2hMA22Jlfc
257. http://www.bizjournals.com/twincities/print-edition/2011/08/19/marco-inc.html
258. http://mashable.com/2011/08/07/startup-employee-perks/
259. http://www.outsideonline.com/outdoor-adventure/best-jobs/More-Best-Places-to-Work-CamelBak-Products-20120801.html
260. http://www.outsideonline.com/outdoor-adventure/best-jobs/Tabar.html
261. http://www.bizjournals.com/twincities/print-edition/2011/08/19/martin-williams-inc.html?page=all
262. http://adage.com/article/special-report-best-places-to-work-2012/undertone-9-ad-age-s-places-work-list/233652/
263. http://www.businessinsider.com/the-25-best-places-to-work-around-the-world-2012-11?op=1
264. http://www.businessinsider.com/the-25-best-places-to-work-around-the-world-2012-11?op=1#ixzz2E8vD2ohm
265. http://blogs.hbr.org/hbr/hewlett/2012/05/attract_and_keep_a-players_wit.html
266. http://blogs.hbr.org/cs/2011/02/secrets_of_positive_feedback.html
267. http://www.bestplacestoworkla.com/index.php?option=com_content&task=view&id=60
268. http://www.washingtonian.com/articles/work-education/washington-offices-with-the-best-coffee-highest-pay-and-more/
269. http://adage.com/article/best-places-to-work/places-work-media-marketing-iprospect/229326/
270. http://www.greatplacetowork.com/2012-best-workplaces/professional-placement-resources
271. http://mashable.com/2011/08/07/startup-employee-perks/
272. http://flavors.me/bwelfel
273. http://www.topworkplaces.com/frontend.php/regional-list/company/chron/st-regis-houston
274. http://www.bizjournals.com/twincities/print-edition/2011/08/19/harbinger-partners-inc.html?page=all

275. http://www.chron.com/news/article/No-5-small-company-Hotze-Health-amp-Wellness-4021026.php
276. http://www.chron.com/business/article/At-Brady-Chapman-Holland-fun-and-achievement-2254152.php
277. http://www.worklifepolicy.org/
278. http://blogs.hbr.org/hbr/hewlett/2012/05/attract_and_keep_a-players_wit.html
279. https://www.mckinseyquarterly.com/Preparing_for_a_new_era_of_knowl edge_work
280. http://www.teleworkresearchnetwork.com/
281. http://money.cnn.com/magazines/fortune/best-companies/2012/benefits/telecommuting.html
282. http://www.citrix.com/site/resources/dynamic/salesdocs/Citrix_Workshift ing_Index_Whitepaper_FINAL.pdf
283. http://www.entrepreneur.com/article/219509
284. http://www.patagonia.com/us/patagonia.go?assetid=1963
285. http://www.mckinsey.com/insights/organization/preparing_for_a_new_er a_of_knowledge_work?p=1
286. http://www.tampabay.com/news/business/workinglife/work-schedule-flexibility-is-a-major-attraction-at-busch-gardens/1226658
287. http://www.brandlearning.com/Blog-articles-And-news/News/BL-Leaps-To-3rd-Place.aspx
288. http://www.oregonbusiness.com/articles/112-march-2012/6795-the-2012-list-top-33-small-companies-to-work-for-in-oregon?start=3#ixzz25HAskUmS
289. http://www.flexjobs.com/jobs/telecommuting-jobs-at-ikea
290. http://theprfreelancer.com/
291. http://management.fortune.cnn.com/2012/05/01/happiness-at-work-fulfillment/
292. http://www.bestplacestoworkla.com/index.php?option=com_content&tas k=view&id=60
293. http://www.bizjournals.com/atlanta/print-edition/2012/09/14/pricewaterhousecoopers-llp.html?page=all
294. http://www.businessweek.com/stories/2006-12-10/smashing-the-clock
295. http://www.virtualvocations.com/blog/telecommuting-news/best-buys-banish-on-telecommuting-much-ado-about-nothing/
296. http://allthingsd.com/20130225/survey-says-despite-yahoo-ban-most-tech-companies-support-work-from-home-for-employees/
297. http://www.inc.com/guides/2010/08/10-things-employees-want.html
298. http://www.edmunds.com/about/press/edmundscom-recognized-as-a-best-place-to-work-by-los-angeles-business-journal.html
299. http://smithfloyd.com
300. http://www.thefiscaltimes.com/Articles/2011/05/19/16-Company-Perks-That-Will-Make-You-Jealous.aspx#page1
301. http://www.bestplacestoworkla.com/index.php?option=com_content&tas k=view&id=60
302. http://www.prnewsonline.com/awards/top-work-places/2012/11/29/2012-top-places-to-work-in-pr-counterpart-international-inc/
303. http://www.mersgoodwill.org/about/jobs
304. http://adage.com/article/best-places-to-work/places-work-marketing-media-orion-trading/229340/
305. http://www.convinceandconvert.com/social-business/social-business-is-about-actions-not-words/?utm_campaign=Argyle%2BSocial-2011-12&utm_medium=Argyle%2BSocial&utm_source=linkedin&utm_term=20 11-12-17-22-41-00

306. http://www.qualitylogoproducts.com/blog/attracting-talent-increasing-company-loyalty/#ixzz23MKMO3Vn
307. http://www.hotstudio.com/thoughts/hot-studio-welcomes-babies-work-new-pilot-program
308. http://www.darden.com/careers/restaurants.asp
309. http://www.jabian.com/news/jabian-named-best-place-to-work-by-atlanta-business-chronicle/
310. http://blog.chron.com/houstonshiring/2011/06/bbs-technologies-named-best-place-to-work-is-hiring/
311. http://www.nytimes.com/2012/04/08/business/phil-libin-of-evernote-on-its-unusual-corporate-culture.html?pagewanted=all&_r=0
312. http://www.chicagobusiness.com/article/20120331/ISSUE02/120329728/why-your-perks-arent-working#ixzz23eQnmYWN
313. http://www.newswala.com/Special-News/Employees-quit-bosses-not-jobs-Survey-19783.html
314. http://www.forbes.com/sites/victorlipman/2012/09/10/10-reasons-why-companies-should-invest-more-in-management-training/
315. http://goodthinkinc.com/the-happiness-advantage/
316. http://www.bizjournals.com/twincities/print-edition/2011/08/19/ecumen.html?page=all
317. http://www.squeezein.com/
318. http://www.colliers.com/TrainingandDevelopment
319. http://www.bizjournals.com/atlanta/print-edition/2011/09/16/accenture.html?page=all
320. http://www.achievemax.com/blog/2009/03/12/the-container-store/
321. http://www.1to1media.com/weblog/2011/07/customer_bliss_jeanne_bliss_we.html
322. http://www.hoarllc.com/News/NewsDetail/20111025.bptw.html
323. www.bizjournals.com/stlouis/
324. http://www.eluta.ca/work-at-monsanto
325. http://www.eluta.ca/work-at-nexen
326. http://www.bizjournals.com/twincities/print-edition/2011/08/19/nina-hale.html?page=all
327. http://www.entrepreneur.com/gptw/index.html
328. http://adage.com/article/special-report-best-places-to-work-2012/horizon-media-10-ad-age-s-places-work-list/233649/
329. http://www.bizjournals.com/portland/print-edition/2012/10/05/xplane-returns-home.html?page=all
330. http://www.amazon.com/The-Seven-Day-Weekend-Changing-Works/dp/1591840260
331. http://www.dailyfinance.com/2011/08/24/companies-that-treat-workers-right-get-good-karma-right-back/
332. http://dvn.com
333. http://www.washingtonian.com/articles/work-education/washington-offices-with-the-best-coffee-highest-pay-and-more/
334. http://www.eluta.ca/top-employer-td-bank
335. http://www.eluta.ca/top-employer-dialog-vancouver
336. http://www.eluta.ca/top-employer-university-of-toronto
337. http://www.eluta.ca/work-at-bcsa
338. http://money.cnn.com/magazines/fortune/best-companies/2012/snapshots/69.html
339. http://www.prnewsonline.com/awards/top-work-places/2012/11/29/2012-top-places-to-work-in-pr-mww/
340. http://www.entrepreneur.com/gptw/93

341. http://www.nreca.coop/press/NewsReleases/Pages/NRECAMakesTheWas hingtonianList.aspx

342. http://www.qbp.com/files/press/QBP_8.8.12.pdf

343. http://www.oregonbusiness.com/articles/82-march-2010/3110-the-2010-100-best-companies-to-work-for-in-oregon

344. http://www.quora.com/Company-Culture/What-companies-are-the-best-examples-of-great-corporate-culture

345. http://www.washingtonian.com/articles/work-education/great-places-to-work-the-list/

346. http://www.eluta.ca/top-employer-westjet

347. https://www.youtube.com/watch

348. http://www.lane4performance.com/PressDetail.aspx?itemid=609&itemTitl e=Lane4+ranked+16th+in+Sunday+Times+100+Best+Companies+2012&s itesectionid=154&sitesectiontitle=Press

349. http://www.outsideonline.com/outdoor-adventure/best-jobs/50-Tabar.html

350. http://www.prweb.com/releases/2011/10/prweb8900078.htm

351. http://www.inc.com/leigh-buchanan/patagonia-founder-yvon-chouinard-15five.html

352. http://www.beready.net/work/nordstrom-the-one-and-only-rule-in-its-employee-handbook

353. http://www.slideshare.net/reed2001/culture-1798664

354. http://www.fastcompany.com/3002382/why-trying-manipulate-employee-motivation-always-backfires

355. http://chiefcustomerofficer.customerbliss.com/2013/01/08/do-your-employee-ideas-see-the-light-of-day/

356. http://www.youtube.com/watch?v=701MOt3_qCk

357. http://culture.infusionsoft.com/preserving-the-core/how-do-you-hire-a-dream-manager/

358. http://www.bizjournals.com/atlanta/print-edition/2011/09/16/brasfield-gorrie.html?page=all

359. http://www.businessinsider.com/the-25-best-places-to-work-around-the-world-2012-11?op=1#ixzz2E8ydwgNI

360. http://www.prnewsonline.com/awards/top-work-places/2012/11/29/2012-top-places-to-work-in-pr-fahlgren-mortine/

361. http://www.bizjournals.com/twincities/print-edition/2011/08/19/the-nerdery.html?page=all

362. http://smithfloyd.com

363. http://www.cbjonline.com/a2labj/supplements/BestPlaceToWork_1208.pd f

364. http://www.innovation.lv/ino2/publications/leonardo_manual/en/www.inn osupport.net/webhelp/wso/index.cfm@fuseactionlearnl_id4287pl_id3561. htm

365. http://fasthorseinc.com/blog/2010/02/24/fast-horse-perks/

366. http://www.bizjournals.com/twincities/print-edition/2011/08/19/weber-shandwick.html?page=all

367. http://www.fastcodesign.com/1663137/how-3m-gave-everyone-days-off-and-created-an-innovation-dynamo

368. http://www.inc.com/top-workplaces/2010/profile/azavea-robert-cheetham.html

369. http://www.businessinsider.com/the-25-best-small-companies-to-work-for-right-now-2012-10?op=1

370. http://www.siemens.com/press/en/pressrelease/?press=/en/pressrelease/2010/corporate_communication/axx20101003.htm

371.   http://www.entrepreneur.com/gptw/58